This Planner belongs to:
_____

A note from Karen:

Hello Life Magician,

Thank you for letting me join you on this year of daily life magic. The reason why it is important to keep a detailed journal like this is because:

1. So much can happen in a year and you will be able to reflect on progress.
2. You will be more mindful about each aspect of your potential daily life magic.
3. You will be focused on you.

This journal is not dated for a reason. There will be days when you forget or are not feeling it for a day, and as much as it is important to keep a log, it is equally as important to give yourself a break. Focus on your positives and the wonderful things you are achieveing and leave the rest to the side. YOU DO NOT HAVE TO FILL IN EVERY BOX, fill in what you want to.

How to use this planner:
1. There are 365 days in this planner, use them as you wish.
2. Complete the vision board early on your journey, it is situated at the back of the planner.
3. Prioritise joy in your life and success is inevitable.
4. Come join us in my Life Magic Mastery with K P Weaver Facebook group and share your progress.

I do hope that this planner navigates you to capturing the magic in every day.

Love always,
Karen

DAILY LIFE MAGIC

DATE:
(S) (M) (T) (W) (T) (F) (S)

JOY LEVEL

TODAY'S INTENTIONS

REMINDER TO:

QUOTE FOR TODAY

INSPIRED THOUGHTS:

TODAY'S PRIORITES:

EXERCISE:

TOTAL MINUTES:	
TOTAL STEPS:	

WATER INTAKE:

MEAL TRACKER:

BREAKFAST:	LUNCH:
DINNER:	SNACKS:

TO CALL OR EMAIL:

MONEY

MANIFESTED:	GRATEFULLY OUT:

TODAY I AM GRATEFUL FOR:

NOTES:

NEXT DAY GET AHEAD

DAILY LIFE MAGIC

DATE:

(S) (M) (T) (W) (T) (F) (S)

JOY LEVEL

TODAY'S INTENTIONS

REMINDER TO:

QUOTE FOR TODAY

INSPIRED THOUGHTS:

TODAY'S PRIORITES:

EXERCISE:

TOTAL MINUTES:	
TOTAL STEPS:	

WATER INTAKE:
◊ ◊ ◊ ◊ ◊ ◊ ◊

MEAL TRACKER:

BREAKFAST:	LUNCH:
DINNER:	SNACKS:

TO CALL OR EMAIL:

MONEY

MANIFESTED:	GRATEFULLY OUT:

TODAY I AM GRATEFUL FOR:

NOTES:

NEXT DAY GET AHEAD

DAILY LIFE MAGIC

DATE:

(S) (M) (T) (W) (T) (F) (S)

JOY LEVEL

TODAY'S INTENTIONS

REMINDER TO:

QUOTE FOR TODAY

TODAY'S PRIORITES:

INSPIRED THOUGHTS:

EXERCISE:

TOTAL MINUTES:	
TOTAL STEPS:	

WATER INTAKE:

◯ ◯ ◯ ◯ ◯ ◯ ◯

MEAL TRACKER:

BREAKFAST:	LUNCH:
DINNER:	SNACKS:

TO CALL OR EMAIL:

MONEY

MANIFESTED:	GRATEFULLY OUT:

TODAY I AM GRATEFUL FOR:

NOTES:

NEXT DAY GET AHEAD

DAILY LIFE MAGIC

DATE:
(S) (M) (T) (W) (T) (F) (S)

JOY LEVEL

TODAY'S INTENTIONS

REMINDER TO:

QUOTE FOR TODAY

TODAY'S PRIORITES:

INSPIRED THOUGHTS:

EXERCISE:

TOTAL MINUTES:	
TOTAL STEPS:	

WATER INTAKE:

○ ○ ○ ○ ○ ○ ○

MEAL TRACKER:

BREAKFAST:	LUNCH:
DINNER:	SNACKS:

TO CALL OR EMAIL:

MONEY

MANIFESTED:	GRATEFULLY OUT:

TODAY I AM GRATEFUL FOR:

NOTES:

NEXT DAY GET AHEAD

DAILY LIFE MAGIC

DATE:

(S) (M) (T) (W) (T) (F) (S)

JOY LEVEL

TODAY'S INTENTIONS

REMINDER TO:

QUOTE FOR TODAY

EXERCISE:

TOTAL MINUTES:	
TOTAL STEPS:	

WATER INTAKE:

○ ○ ○ ○ ○ ○ ○

MEAL TRACKER:

BREAKFAST:	LUNCH:
DINNER:	SNACKS:

TODAY'S PRIORITES:

TO CALL OR EMAIL:

INSPIRED THOUGHTS:

MONEY

MANIFESTED:	GRATEFULLY OUT:

TODAY I AM GRATEFUL FOR:

NOTES:

NEXT DAY GET AHEAD

DAILY LIFE MAGIC

DATE:
(S)(M)(T)(W)(T)(F)(S)

JOY LEVEL

TODAY'S INTENTIONS

REMINDER TO:

QUOTE FOR TODAY

INSPIRED THOUGHTS :

TODAY'S PRIORITES:

EXERCISE:

TOTAL MINUTES:	
TOTAL STEPS:	

WATER INTAKE:

MEAL TRACKER:

BREAKFAST:	LUNCH:
DINNER:	SNACKS:

TO CALL OR EMAIL:

MONEY

MANIFESTED:	GRATEFULLY OUT:

TODAY I AM GRATEFUL FOR:

NOTES:

NEXT DAY GET AHEAD

DAILY LIFE MAGIC

DATE:

(S) (M) (T) (W) (T) (F) (S)

JOY LEVEL

TODAY'S INTENTIONS

REMINDER TO:

QUOTE FOR TODAY

INSPIRED THOUGHTS:

TODAY'S PRIORITES:

EXERCISE:

TOTAL MINUTES:	
TOTAL STEPS:	

WATER INTAKE:

MEAL TRACKER:

BREAKFAST:	LUNCH:
DINNER:	SNACKS:

TO CALL OR EMAIL:

MONEY

MANIFESTED:	GRATEFULLY OUT:

TODAY I AM GRATEFUL FOR:

NOTES:

NEXT DAY GET AHEAD

DAILY LIFE MAGIC

DATE:
(S) (M) (T) (W) (T) (F) (S)

JOY LEVEL

TODAY'S INTENTIONS

REMINDER TO:

QUOTE FOR TODAY

INSPIRED THOUGHTS :

TODAY'S PRIORITES:

EXERCISE:

TOTAL MINUTES:	
TOTAL STEPS:	

WATER INTAKE:

MEAL TRACKER:

BREAKFAST:	LUNCH:
DINNER:	SNACKS:

TO CALL OR EMAIL:

MONEY

MANIFESTED:	GRATEFULLY OUT:

TODAY I AM GRATEFUL FOR:

NOTES:

NEXT DAY GET AHEAD

DAILY LIFE MAGIC

DATE:

(S) (M) (T) (W) (T) (F) (S)

JOY LEVEL

TODAY'S INTENTIONS

REMINDER TO:

QUOTE FOR TODAY

TODAY'S PRIORITES:

INSPIRED THOUGHTS:

EXERCISE:

TOTAL MINUTES:	
TOTAL STEPS:	

WATER INTAKE:

○ ○ ○ ○ ○ ○ ○

MEAL TRACKER:

BREAKFAST:	LUNCH:
DINNER:	SNACKS:

TO CALL OR EMAIL:

MONEY

MANIFESTED:	GRATEFULLY OUT:

TODAY I AM GRATEFUL FOR:

NOTES:

NEXT DAY GET AHEAD

DAILY LIFE MAGIC

DATE:

(S) (M) (T) (W) (T) (F) (S)

JOY LEVEL

TODAY'S INTENTIONS

REMINDER TO:

QUOTE FOR TODAY

INSPIRED THOUGHTS :

TODAY'S PRIORITES:

EXERCISE:

TOTAL MINUTES:	
TOTAL STEPS:	

WATER INTAKE:

◯ ◯ ◯ ◯ ◯ ◯ ◯

MEAL TRACKER:

TO CALL OR EMAIL:

MONEY

BREAKFAST:	LUNCH:
DINNER:	SNACKS:

MANIFESTED:	GRATEFULLY OUT:

TODAY I AM GRATEFUL FOR:

NOTES:

NEXT DAY GET AHEAD

DAILY LIFE MAGIC

DATE:
S M T W T F S

JOY LEVEL

QUOTE FOR TODAY

TODAY'S INTENTIONS

REMINDER TO:

EXERCISE:

TOTAL MINUTES:	
TOTAL STEPS:	

WATER INTAKE:

○ ○ ○ ○ ○ ○ ○ ○

TODAY'S PRIORITES:

INSPIRED THOUGHTS :

MEAL TRACKER:

BREAKFAST:	LUNCH:
DINNER:	SNACKS:

TO CALL OR EMAIL:

MONEY

MANIFESTED:	GRATEFULLY OUT:

TODAY I AM GRATEFUL FOR:

NOTES:

NEXT DAY GET AHEAD

DAILY LIFE MAGIC

DATE:

(S) (M) (T) (W) (T) (F) (S)

JOY LEVEL

TODAY'S INTENTIONS

REMINDER TO:

QUOTE FOR TODAY

INSPIRED THOUGHTS :

TODAY'S PRIORITES:

EXERCISE:

TOTAL MINUTES:	
TOTAL STEPS:	

WATER INTAKE:

○ ○ ○ ○ ○ ○ ○

MEAL TRACKER:

BREAKFAST:	LUNCH:
DINNER:	SNACKS:

TO CALL OR EMAIL:

MONEY

MANIFESTED:	GRATEFULLY OUT:

TODAY I AM GRATEFUL FOR:

NOTES:

NEXT DAY GET AHEAD

DAILY LIFE MAGIC

DATE:

(S) (M) (T) (W) (T) (F) (S)

JOY LEVEL

😃 🙂 😐 🙁 😢

QUOTE FOR TODAY

TODAY'S INTENTIONS

REMINDER TO:

INSPIRED THOUGHTS :

TODAY'S PRIORITES:

EXERCISE:

TOTAL MINUTES:	
TOTAL STEPS:	

WATER INTAKE:

💧💧💧💧💧💧💧

MEAL TRACKER:

BREAKFAST:	LUNCH:
DINNER:	SNACKS:

TO CALL OR EMAIL:

MONEY

MANIFESTED:	GRATEFULLY OUT:

TODAY I AM GRATEFUL FOR:

NOTES:

NEXT DAY GET AHEAD

DAILY LIFE MAGIC

DATE:

(S) (M) (T) (W) (T) (F) (S)

JOY LEVEL

TODAY'S INTENTIONS

REMINDER TO:

QUOTE FOR TODAY

INSPIRED THOUGHTS :

TODAY'S PRIORITES:

EXERCISE:

TOTAL MINUTES:	
TOTAL STEPS:	

WATER INTAKE:

MEAL TRACKER:

BREAKFAST:	LUNCH:
DINNER:	SNACKS:

TO CALL OR EMAIL:

MONEY

MANIFESTED:	GRATEFULLY OUT:

TODAY I AM GRATEFUL FOR:

NOTES:

NEXT DAY GET AHEAD

DAILY LIFE MAGIC

DATE:

(S) (M) (T) (W) (T) (F) (S)

JOY LEVEL

TODAY'S INTENTIONS

REMINDER TO:

QUOTE FOR TODAY

TODAY'S PRIORITES:

INSPIRED THOUGHTS :

EXERCISE:

TOTAL MINUTES:	
TOTAL STEPS:	

WATER INTAKE:

MEAL TRACKER:

BREAKFAST:	LUNCH:
DINNER:	SNACKS:

TO CALL OR EMAIL:

MONEY

MANIFESTED:	GRATEFULLY OUT:

TODAY I AM GRATEFUL FOR:

NOTES:

NEXT DAY GET AHEAD

DAILY LIFE MAGIC

DATE:

JOY LEVEL

TODAY'S INTENTIONS

REMINDER TO:

QUOTE FOR TODAY

INSPIRED THOUGHTS :

TODAY'S PRIORITES:

EXERCISE:

TOTAL MINUTES:	
TOTAL STEPS:	

WATER INTAKE:
○ ○ ○ ○ ○ ○ ○

MEAL TRACKER:

BREAKFAST:	LUNCH:
DINNER:	SNACKS:

TO CALL OR EMAIL:

MONEY

MANIFESTED:	GRATEFULLY OUT:

TODAY I AM GRATEFUL FOR:

NOTES:

NEXT DAY GET AHEAD

DAILY LIFE MAGIC

DATE:

(S) (M) (T) (W) (T) (F) (S)

JOY LEVEL

TODAY'S INTENTIONS

REMINDER TO:

QUOTE FOR TODAY

TODAY'S PRIORITES:

INSPIRED THOUGHTS :

EXERCISE:

TOTAL MINUTES:	
TOTAL STEPS:	

WATER INTAKE:

MEAL TRACKER:

BREAKFAST:	LUNCH:
DINNER:	SNACKS:

TO CALL OR EMAIL:

MONEY

MANIFESTED:	GRATEFULLY OUT:

TODAY I AM GRATEFUL FOR:

NOTES:

NEXT DAY GET AHEAD

DAILY LIFE MAGIC

DATE:
(S) (M) (T) (W) (T) (F) (S)

JOY LEVEL

TODAY'S INTENTIONS

REMINDER TO:

QUOTE FOR TODAY

TODAY'S PRIORITES:

INSPIRED THOUGHTS :

EXERCISE:

TOTAL MINUTES:	
TOTAL STEPS:	

WATER INTAKE:

◊ ◊ ◊ ◊ ◊ ◊ ◊

MEAL TRACKER:

BREAKFAST:	LUNCH:
DINNER:	SNACKS:

TO CALL OR EMAIL:

MONEY

MANIFESTED:	GRATEFULLY OUT:

TODAY I AM GRATEFUL FOR:

NOTES:

NEXT DAY GET AHEAD

DAILY LIFE MAGIC

DATE:

Ⓢ Ⓜ Ⓣ Ⓦ Ⓣ Ⓕ Ⓢ

JOY LEVEL

TODAY'S INTENTIONS

REMINDER TO:

QUOTE FOR TODAY

INSPIRED THOUGHTS :

TODAY'S PRIORITES:

EXERCISE:

TOTAL MINUTES:	
TOTAL STEPS:	

WATER INTAKE:

◊ ◊ ◊ ◊ ◊ ◊ ◊

MEAL TRACKER:

BREAKFAST:	LUNCH:
DINNER:	SNACKS:

TO CALL OR EMAIL:

MONEY

MANIFESTED:	GRATEFULLY OUT:

TODAY I AM GRATEFUL FOR:

NOTES:

NEXT DAY GET AHEAD

DAILY LIFE MAGIC

DATE:

(S) (M) (T) (W) (T) (F) (S)

JOY LEVEL

TODAY'S INTENTIONS

REMINDER TO:

QUOTE FOR TODAY

TODAY'S PRIORITES:

INSPIRED THOUGHTS :

EXERCISE:

TOTAL MINUTES:	
TOTAL STEPS:	

WATER INTAKE:

MEAL TRACKER:

BREAKFAST:	LUNCH:
DINNER:	SNACKS:

TO CALL OR EMAIL:

MONEY

MANIFESTED:	GRATEFULLY OUT:

TODAY I AM GRATEFUL FOR:

NOTES:

NEXT DAY GET AHEAD

DAILY LIFE MAGIC

DATE:

(S) (M) (T) (W) (T) (F) (S)

JOY LEVEL

TODAY'S INTENTIONS

REMINDER TO:

QUOTE FOR TODAY

INSPIRED THOUGHTS:

TODAY'S PRIORITES:

EXERCISE:

TOTAL MINUTES:	
TOTAL STEPS:	

WATER INTAKE:

◯ ◯ ◯ ◯ ◯ ◯ ◯

MEAL TRACKER:

BREAKFAST:	LUNCH:
DINNER:	SNACKS:

TO CALL OR EMAIL:

MONEY

MANIFESTED:	GRATEFULLY OUT:

TODAY I AM GRATEFUL FOR:

NOTES:

NEXT DAY GET AHEAD

DAILY LIFE MAGIC

DATE:

(S) (M) (T) (W) (T) (F) (S)

JOY LEVEL

TODAY'S INTENTIONS

REMINDER TO:

QUOTE FOR TODAY

TODAY'S PRIORITES:

INSPIRED THOUGHTS :

EXERCISE:

TOTAL MINUTES:	
TOTAL STEPS:	

WATER INTAKE:

MEAL TRACKER:

BREAKFAST:	LUNCH:
DINNER:	SNACKS:

TO CALL OR EMAIL:

MONEY

MANIFESTED:	GRATEFULLY OUT:

TODAY I AM GRATEFUL FOR:

NOTES:

NEXT DAY GET AHEAD

DAILY LIFE MAGIC

DATE:

(S) (M) (T) (W) (T) (F) (S)

JOY LEVEL

TODAY'S INTENTIONS

REMINDER TO:

QUOTE FOR TODAY

TODAY'S PRIORITES:

INSPIRED THOUGHTS:

EXERCISE:

TOTAL MINUTES:	
TOTAL STEPS:	

WATER INTAKE:

MEAL TRACKER:

BREAKFAST:	LUNCH:
DINNER:	SNACKS:

TO CALL OR EMAIL:

MONEY

MANIFESTED:	GRATEFULLY OUT:

TODAY I AM GRATEFUL FOR:

NOTES:

NEXT DAY GET AHEAD

DAILY LIFE MAGIC

DATE:
Ⓢ Ⓜ Ⓣ Ⓦ Ⓣ Ⓕ Ⓢ

JOY LEVEL

TODAY'S INTENTIONS

REMINDER TO:

QUOTE FOR TODAY

INSPIRED THOUGHTS:

TODAY'S PRIORITES:

EXERCISE:

TOTAL MINUTES:	
TOTAL STEPS:	

WATER INTAKE:
○ ○ ○ ○ ○ ○ ○

MEAL TRACKER:

BREAKFAST:	LUNCH:
DINNER:	SNACKS:

TO CALL OR EMAIL:

MONEY

MANIFESTED:	GRATEFULLY OUT:

TODAY I AM GRATEFUL FOR:

NOTES:

NEXT DAY GET AHEAD

DAILY LIFE MAGIC

DATE:

Ⓢ Ⓜ Ⓣ Ⓦ Ⓣ Ⓕ Ⓢ

JOY LEVEL

TODAY'S INTENTIONS

REMINDER TO:

QUOTE FOR TODAY

INSPIRED THOUGHTS :

TODAY'S PRIORITES:

EXERCISE:

TOTAL MINUTES:	
TOTAL STEPS:	

WATER INTAKE:

◯ ◯ ◯ ◯ ◯ ◯ ◯

MEAL TRACKER:

TO CALL OR EMAIL:

MONEY

BREAKFAST:	LUNCH:
DINNER:	SNACKS:

MANIFESTED:	GRATEFULLY OUT:

TODAY I AM GRATEFUL FOR:

NOTES:

NEXT DAY GET AHEAD

DAILY LIFE MAGIC

DATE:
(S) (M) (T) (W) (T) (F) (S)

JOY LEVEL

TODAY'S INTENTIONS

REMINDER TO:

QUOTE FOR TODAY

TODAY'S PRIORITES:

INSPIRED THOUGHTS:

EXERCISE:

TOTAL MINUTES:	
TOTAL STEPS:	

WATER INTAKE:
○○○○○○○

MEAL TRACKER:

BREAKFAST:	LUNCH:
DINNER:	SNACKS:

TO CALL OR EMAIL:

MONEY

MANIFESTED:	GRATEFULLY OUT:

TODAY I AM GRATEFUL FOR:

NOTES:

NEXT DAY GET AHEAD

DAILY LIFE MAGIC

DATE:

(S) (M) (T) (W) (T) (F) (S)

JOY LEVEL

😊 🙂 😐 🙁 😢

QUOTE FOR TODAY

TODAY'S INTENTIONS

REMINDER TO:

INSPIRED THOUGHTS:

TODAY'S PRIORITES:

EXERCISE:

TOTAL MINUTES:	
TOTAL STEPS:	

WATER INTAKE:

💧💧💧💧💧💧💧

MEAL TRACKER:

BREAKFAST:	LUNCH:
DINNER:	SNACKS:

TO CALL OR EMAIL:

MONEY

MANIFESTED:	GRATEFULLY OUT:

TODAY I AM GRATEFUL FOR:

NOTES:

NEXT DAY GET AHEAD

DAILY LIFE MAGIC

DATE:

(S) (T) (T)

JOY LEVEL

TODAY'S INTENTIONS

REMINDER TO:

QUOTE FOR TODAY

INSPIRED THOUGHTS:

TODAY'S PRIORITES:

EXERCISE:

TOTAL MINUTES:	
TOTAL STEPS:	

WATER INTAKE:
○ ○ ○ ○ ○ ○ ○

MEAL TRACKER:

BREAKFAST:	LUNCH:
DINNER:	SNACKS:

TO CALL OR EMAIL:

MONEY

MANIFESTED:	GRATEFULLY OUT:

TODAY I AM GRATEFUL FOR:

NOTES:

NEXT DAY GET AHEAD

DAILY LIFE MAGIC

DATE:

Ⓢ Ⓜ Ⓣ Ⓦ Ⓣ Ⓕ Ⓢ

JOY LEVEL

TODAY'S INTENTIONS

REMINDER TO:

QUOTE FOR TODAY

TODAY'S PRIORITIES:

INSPIRED THOUGHTS:

EXERCISE:

TOTAL MINUTES:	
TOTAL STEPS:	

WATER INTAKE:

○ ○ ○ ○ ○ ○ ○

MEAL TRACKER:

BREAKFAST:	LUNCH:
DINNER:	SNACKS:

TO CALL OR EMAIL:

MONEY

MANIFESTED:	GRATEFULLY OUT:

TODAY I AM GRATEFUL FOR:

NOTES:

NEXT DAY GET AHEAD

DAILY LIFE MAGIC

DATE:

(S) (M) (T) (W) (T) (F) (S)

JOY LEVEL

TODAY'S INTENTIONS

REMINDER TO:

QUOTE FOR TODAY

INSPIRED THOUGHTS :

TODAY'S PRIORITES:

EXERCISE:

TOTAL MINUTES:	
TOTAL STEPS:	

WATER INTAKE:

○ ○ ○ ○ ○ ○ ○

MEAL TRACKER:

BREAKFAST:	LUNCH:
DINNER:	SNACKS:

TO CALL OR EMAIL:

MONEY

MANIFESTED:	GRATEFULLY OUT:

TODAY I AM GRATEFUL FOR:

NOTES:

NEXT DAY GET AHEAD

DAILY LIFE MAGIC

DATE:
(S) (M) (T) (W) (T) (F) (S)

JOY LEVEL

TODAY'S INTENTIONS

REMINDER TO:

QUOTE FOR TODAY

INSPIRED THOUGHTS:

TODAY'S PRIORITES:

EXERCISE:

TOTAL MINUTES:	
TOTAL STEPS:	

WATER INTAKE:

MEAL TRACKER:

BREAKFAST:	LUNCH:
DINNER:	SNACKS:

TO CALL OR EMAIL:

MONEY

MANIFESTED:	GRATEFULLY OUT:

TODAY I AM GRATEFUL FOR:

NOTES:

NEXT DAY GET AHEAD

DAILY LIFE MAGIC

DATE:
Ⓢ Ⓜ Ⓣ Ⓦ Ⓣ Ⓕ Ⓢ

JOY LEVEL

TODAY'S INTENTIONS

REMINDER TO:

QUOTE FOR TODAY

TODAY'S PRIORITES:

INSPIRED THOUGHTS:

EXERCISE:

TOTAL MINUTES:	
TOTAL STEPS:	

WATER INTAKE:
💧💧💧💧💧💧💧

MEAL TRACKER:

BREAKFAST:	LUNCH:
DINNER:	SNACKS:

TO CALL OR EMAIL:

MONEY

MANIFESTED:	GRATEFULLY OUT:

TODAY I AM GRATEFUL FOR:

NOTES:

NEXT DAY GET AHEAD

DAILY LIFE MAGIC

DATE:

(S) (M) (T) (W) (T) (F) (S)

JOY LEVEL

TODAY'S INTENTIONS

REMINDER TO:

QUOTE FOR TODAY

INSPIRED THOUGHTS:

TODAY'S PRIORITES:

EXERCISE:

TOTAL MINUTES:	
TOTAL STEPS:	

WATER INTAKE:

MEAL TRACKER:

BREAKFAST:	LUNCH:
DINNER:	SNACKS:

TO CALL OR EMAIL:

MONEY

MANIFESTED:	GRATEFULLY OUT:

TODAY I AM GRATEFUL FOR:

NOTES:

NEXT DAY GET AHEAD

DAILY LIFE MAGIC

DATE:

JOY LEVEL

 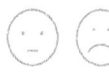

TODAY'S INTENTIONS

REMINDER TO:

QUOTE FOR TODAY

INSPIRED THOUGHTS:

TODAY'S PRIORITES:

EXERCISE:

TOTAL MINUTES:	
TOTAL STEPS:	

WATER INTAKE:

○ ○ ○ ○ ○ ○ ○

MEAL TRACKER:

BREAKFAST:	LUNCH:
DINNER:	SNACKS:

TO CALL OR EMAIL:

MONEY

MANIFESTED:	GRATEFULLY OUT:

TODAY I AM GRATEFUL FOR:

NOTES:

NEXT DAY GET AHEAD

DAILY LIFE MAGIC

DATE:

(S) (M) (T) (W) (T) (F) (S)

JOY LEVEL

TODAY'S INTENTIONS

REMINDER TO:

QUOTE FOR TODAY

INSPIRED THOUGHTS :

TODAY'S PRIORITES:

EXERCISE:

TOTAL MINUTES:	
TOTAL STEPS:	

WATER INTAKE:

MEAL TRACKER:

BREAKFAST:	LUNCH:
DINNER:	SNACKS:

TO CALL OR EMAIL:

MONEY

MANIFESTED:	GRATEFULLY OUT:

TODAY I AM GRATEFUL FOR:

NOTES:

NEXT DAY GET AHEAD

DAILY LIFE MAGIC

DATE:
(S) (M) (T) (W) (T) (F) (S)

JOY LEVEL

TODAY'S INTENTIONS

REMINDER TO:

QUOTE FOR TODAY

INSPIRED THOUGHTS :

TODAY'S PRIORITES:

EXERCISE:

TOTAL MINUTES:	
TOTAL STEPS:	

WATER INTAKE:

◯ ◯ ◯ ◯ ◯ ◯ ◯

MEAL TRACKER:

BREAKFAST:	LUNCH:
DINNER:	SNACKS:

TO CALL OR EMAIL:

MONEY

MANIFESTED:	GRATEFULLY OUT:

TODAY I AM GRATEFUL FOR:

NOTES:

NEXT DAY GET AHEAD

DAILY LIFE MAGIC

DATE:

(S) (M) (T) (W) (T) (F) (S)

JOY LEVEL

QUOTE FOR TODAY

EXERCISE:

TOTAL MINUTES:	
TOTAL STEPS:	

WATER INTAKE:

○ ○ ○ ○ ○ ○ ○

MEAL TRACKER:

BREAKFAST:	LUNCH:
DINNER:	SNACKS:

TODAY I AM GRATEFUL FOR:

TODAY'S INTENTIONS

TODAY'S PRIORITIES:

TO CALL OR EMAIL:

NOTES:

REMINDER TO:

INSPIRED THOUGHTS:

MONEY

MANIFESTED:	GRATEFULLY OUT:

NEXT DAY GET AHEAD

DAILY LIFE MAGIC

DATE:

(S) (M) (T) (W) (T) (F) (S)

JOY LEVEL

TODAY'S INTENTIONS

REMINDER TO:

QUOTE FOR TODAY

INSPIRED THOUGHTS :

TODAY'S PRIORITES:

EXERCISE:

TOTAL MINUTES:	
TOTAL STEPS:	

WATER INTAKE:

MEAL TRACKER:

BREAKFAST:	LUNCH:
DINNER:	SNACKS:

TO CALL OR EMAIL:

MONEY

MANIFESTED:	GRATEFULLY OUT:

TODAY I AM GRATEFUL FOR:

NOTES:

NEXT DAY GET AHEAD

DAILY LIFE MAGIC

DATE:
(S) (M) (T) (W) (T) (F) (S)

JOY LEVEL

TODAY'S INTENTIONS

REMINDER TO:

QUOTE FOR TODAY

TODAY'S PRIORITES:

INSPIRED THOUGHTS:

EXERCISE:

TOTAL MINUTES:	
TOTAL STEPS:	

WATER INTAKE:

MEAL TRACKER:

BREAKFAST:	LUNCH:
DINNER:	SNACKS:

TO CALL OR EMAIL:

MONEY

MANIFESTED:	GRATEFULLY OUT:

TODAY I AM GRATEFUL FOR:

NOTES:

NEXT DAY GET AHEAD

DAILY LIFE MAGIC

DATE:

(S) (M) (T) (W) (T) (F) (S)

JOY LEVEL

TODAY'S INTENTIONS

REMINDER TO:

QUOTE FOR TODAY

EXERCISE:

TOTAL MINUTES:	
TOTAL STEPS:	

WATER INTAKE:
○ ○ ○ ○ ○ ○ ○

MEAL TRACKER:

BREAKFAST:	LUNCH:
DINNER:	SNACKS:

TODAY'S PRIORITIES:

TO CALL OR EMAIL:

INSPIRED THOUGHTS :

MONEY

MANIFESTED:	GRATEFULLY OUT:

TODAY I AM GRATEFUL FOR:

NOTES:

NEXT DAY GET AHEAD

DAILY LIFE MAGIC

DATE:
(S) (M) (T) (W) (T) (F) (S)

JOY LEVEL

TODAY'S INTENTIONS

REMINDER TO:

QUOTE FOR TODAY

TODAY'S PRIORITES:

INSPIRED THOUGHTS :

EXERCISE:

TOTAL MINUTES:	
TOTAL STEPS:	

WATER INTAKE:

MEAL TRACKER:

BREAKFAST:	LUNCH:
DINNER:	SNACKS:

TO CALL OR EMAIL:

MONEY

MANIFESTED:	GRATEFULLY OUT:

TODAY I AM GRATEFUL FOR:

NOTES:

NEXT DAY GET AHEAD

DAILY LIFE MAGIC

DATE:
S M T W T F S

JOY LEVEL

TODAY'S INTENTIONS

REMINDER TO:

QUOTE FOR TODAY

INSPIRED THOUGHTS :

TODAY'S PRIORITES:

EXERCISE:

TOTAL MINUTES:	
TOTAL STEPS:	

WATER INTAKE:

◊ ◊ ◊ ◊ ◊ ◊ ◊

MEAL TRACKER:

BREAKFAST:	LUNCH:
DINNER:	SNACKS:

TO CALL OR EMAIL:

MONEY

MANIFESTED:	GRATEFULLY OUT:

TODAY I AM GRATEFUL FOR:

NOTES:

NEXT DAY GET AHEAD

DAILY LIFE MAGIC

DATE:
(S) (M) (T) (W) (T) (F) (S)

JOY LEVEL

TODAY'S INTENTIONS

REMINDER TO:

QUOTE FOR TODAY

INSPIRED THOUGHTS:

TODAY'S PRIORITES:

EXERCISE:

TOTAL MINUTES:	
TOTAL STEPS:	

WATER INTAKE:

MEAL TRACKER:

BREAKFAST:	LUNCH:
DINNER:	SNACKS:

TO CALL OR EMAIL:

MONEY

MANIFESTED:	GRATEFULLY OUT:

TODAY I AM GRATEFUL FOR:

NOTES:

NEXT DAY GET AHEAD

DAILY LIFE MAGIC

DATE:

Ⓢ Ⓜ Ⓣ Ⓦ Ⓣ Ⓕ Ⓢ

JOY LEVEL

TODAY'S INTENTIONS

REMINDER TO:

QUOTE FOR TODAY

INSPIRED THOUGHTS :

TODAY'S PRIORITES:

EXERCISE:

TOTAL MINUTES:	
TOTAL STEPS:	

WATER INTAKE:

MEAL TRACKER:

BREAKFAST:	LUNCH:
DINNER:	SNACKS:

TO CALL OR EMAIL:

MONEY

MANIFESTED:	GRATEFULLY OUT:

TODAY I AM GRATEFUL FOR:

NOTES:

NEXT DAY GET AHEAD

DAILY LIFE MAGIC

DATE:

(S) (M) (T) (W) (T) (F) (S)

JOY LEVEL

TODAY'S INTENTIONS

REMINDER TO:

QUOTE FOR TODAY

TODAY'S PRIORITES:

INSPIRED THOUGHTS:

EXERCISE:

TOTAL MINUTES:	
TOTAL STEPS:	

WATER INTAKE:

MEAL TRACKER:

BREAKFAST:	LUNCH:
DINNER:	SNACKS:

TO CALL OR EMAIL:

MONEY

MANIFESTED:	GRATEFULLY OUT:

TODAY I AM GRATEFUL FOR:

NOTES:

NEXT DAY GET AHEAD

DAILY LIFE MAGIC

DATE:

(S) (M)(T)(W)(T)(F)(S)

JOY LEVEL

😀 🙂 😐 🙁 😢

QUOTE FOR TODAY

TODAY'S INTENTIONS

REMINDER TO:

INSPIRED THOUGHTS :

TODAY'S PRIORITES:

EXERCISE:

TOTAL MINUTES:	
TOTAL STEPS:	

WATER INTAKE:

💧💧💧💧💧💧💧

MEAL TRACKER:

BREAKFAST:	LUNCH:
DINNER:	SNACKS:

TO CALL OR EMAIL:

MONEY

MANIFESTED:	GRATEFULLY OUT:

TODAY I AM GRATEFUL FOR:

NOTES:

NEXT DAY GET AHEAD

DAILY LIFE MAGIC

DATE:
Ⓢ Ⓜ Ⓣ Ⓦ Ⓣ Ⓕ Ⓢ

JOY LEVEL

TODAY'S INTENTIONS

REMINDER TO:

QUOTE FOR TODAY

INSPIRED THOUGHTS :

TODAY'S PRIORITES:

EXERCISE:

TOTAL MINUTES:	
TOTAL STEPS:	

WATER INTAKE:
💧 💧 💧 💧 💧 💧 💧

MEAL TRACKER:

BREAKFAST:	LUNCH:
DINNER:	SNACKS:

TO CALL OR EMAIL:

MONEY

MANIFESTED:	GRATEFULLY OUT:

TODAY I AM GRATEFUL FOR:

NOTES:

NEXT DAY GET AHEAD

DAILY LIFE MAGIC

DATE:

(S) (M) (T) (W) (T) (F) (S)

JOY LEVEL

TODAY'S INTENTIONS

REMINDER TO:

QUOTE FOR TODAY

INSPIRED THOUGHTS :

TODAY'S PRIORITES:

EXERCISE:

TOTAL MINUTES:	
TOTAL STEPS:	

WATER INTAKE:

MEAL TRACKER:

TO CALL OR EMAIL:

MONEY

BREAKFAST:	LUNCH:
DINNER:	SNACKS:

MANIFESTED:	GRATEFULLY OUT:

TODAY I AM GRATEFUL FOR:

NOTES:

NEXT DAY GET AHEAD

DAILY LIFE MAGIC

DATE:

(S) (M) (T) (W) (T) (F) (S)

JOY LEVEL

TODAY'S INTENTIONS

REMINDER TO:

QUOTE FOR TODAY

INSPIRED THOUGHTS:

TODAY'S PRIORITES:

EXERCISE:

TOTAL MINUTES:	
TOTAL STEPS:	

WATER INTAKE:

MEAL TRACKER:

BREAKFAST:	LUNCH:
DINNER:	SNACKS:

TO CALL OR EMAIL:

MONEY

MANIFESTED:	GRATEFULLY OUT:

TODAY I AM GRATEFUL FOR:

NOTES:

NEXT DAY GET AHEAD

DAILY LIFE MAGIC

DATE:

Ⓢ Ⓜ Ⓣ Ⓦ Ⓣ Ⓕ Ⓢ

| JOY LEVEL | TODAY'S INTENTIONS | REMINDER TO: |

QUOTE FOR TODAY

INSPIRED THOUGHTS :

TODAY'S PRIORITES:

EXERCISE:

TOTAL MINUTES:	
TOTAL STEPS:	

WATER INTAKE:

○ ○ ○ ○ ○ ○ ○

MEAL TRACKER:

TO CALL OR EMAIL:

MONEY

BREAKFAST:	LUNCH:
DINNER:	SNACKS:

MANIFESTED:	GRATEFULLY OUT:

TODAY I AM GRATEFUL FOR:

NOTES:

NEXT DAY GET AHEAD

DAILY LIFE MAGIC

DATE:

(S) (M) (T) (W) (T) (F) (S)

JOY LEVEL

TODAY'S INTENTIONS

REMINDER TO:

QUOTE FOR TODAY

TODAY'S PRIORITES:

INSPIRED THOUGHTS:

EXERCISE:

TOTAL MINUTES:	
TOTAL STEPS:	

WATER INTAKE:

MEAL TRACKER:

BREAKFAST:	LUNCH:
DINNER:	SNACKS:

TO CALL OR EMAIL:

MONEY

MANIFESTED:	GRATEFULLY OUT:

TODAY I AM GRATEFUL FOR:

NOTES:

NEXT DAY GET AHEAD

DAILY LIFE MAGIC

DATE:

S M W F

JOY LEVEL

TODAY'S INTENTIONS

REMINDER TO:

QUOTE FOR TODAY

INSPIRED THOUGHTS :

TODAY'S PRIORITES:

EXERCISE:

| TOTAL MINUTES: | |
| TOTAL STEPS: | |

WATER INTAKE:

○ ○ ○ ○ ○ ○ ○

MEAL TRACKER:

| BREAKFAST: | LUNCH: |
| DINNER: | SNACKS: |

TO CALL OR EMAIL:

MONEY

| MANIFESTED: | GRATEFULLY OUT: |

TODAY I AM GRATEFUL FOR:

NOTES:

NEXT DAY GET AHEAD

DAILY LIFE MAGIC

DATE:

(S) (M) (T) (W) (T) (F) (S)

JOY LEVEL

TODAY'S INTENTIONS

REMINDER TO:

QUOTE FOR TODAY

INSPIRED THOUGHTS :

TODAY'S PRIORITES:

EXERCISE:

TOTAL MINUTES:	
TOTAL STEPS:	

WATER INTAKE:

MEAL TRACKER:

BREAKFAST:	LUNCH:
DINNER:	SNACKS:

TO CALL OR EMAIL:

MONEY

MANIFESTED:	GRATEFULLY OUT:

TODAY I AM GRATEFUL FOR:

NOTES:

NEXT DAY GET AHEAD

DAILY LIFE MAGIC

DATE:

S M T W T F S

JOY LEVEL

TODAY'S INTENTIONS

REMINDER TO:

QUOTE FOR TODAY

INSPIRED THOUGHTS :

TODAY'S PRIORITES:

EXERCISE:

TOTAL MINUTES:	
TOTAL STEPS:	

WATER INTAKE:

MEAL TRACKER:

BREAKFAST:	LUNCH:
DINNER:	SNACKS:

TO CALL OR EMAIL:

MONEY

MANIFESTED:	GRATEFULLY OUT:

TODAY I AM GRATEFUL FOR:

NOTES:

NEXT DAY GET AHEAD

DAILY LIFE MAGIC

DATE:
(S) (M) (T) (W) (T) (F) (S)

JOY LEVEL

TODAY'S INTENTIONS

REMINDER TO:

QUOTE FOR TODAY

TODAY'S PRIORITES:

INSPIRED THOUGHTS:

EXERCISE:

TOTAL MINUTES:	
TOTAL STEPS:	

WATER INTAKE:

MEAL TRACKER:

BREAKFAST:	LUNCH:
DINNER:	SNACKS:

TO CALL OR EMAIL:

MONEY

MANIFESTED:	GRATEFULLY OUT:

TODAY I AM GRATEFUL FOR:

NOTES:

NEXT DAY GET AHEAD

DAILY LIFE MAGIC

DATE:
(S) (M) (T) (W) (T) (F) (S)

JOY LEVEL

TODAY'S INTENTIONS

REMINDER TO:

QUOTE FOR TODAY

INSPIRED THOUGHTS :

TODAY'S PRIORITES:

EXERCISE:

TOTAL MINUTES:	
TOTAL STEPS:	

WATER INTAKE:
◯ ◯ ◯ ◯ ◯ ◯ ◯

MEAL TRACKER:

BREAKFAST:	LUNCH:
DINNER:	SNACKS:

TO CALL OR EMAIL:

MONEY

MANIFESTED:	GRATEFULLY OUT:

TODAY I AM GRATEFUL FOR:

NOTES:

NEXT DAY GET AHEAD

DAILY LIFE MAGIC

DATE:

(S) (M) (T) (W) (T) (F) (S)

JOY LEVEL

😊 🙂 😐 🙁 😢

TODAY'S INTENTIONS

REMINDER TO:

QUOTE FOR TODAY

TODAY'S PRIORITES:

INSPIRED THOUGHTS:

EXERCISE:

TOTAL MINUTES:	
TOTAL STEPS:	

WATER INTAKE:

💧 💧 💧 💧 💧 💧 💧

MEAL TRACKER:

BREAKFAST:	LUNCH:
DINNER:	SNACKS:

TO CALL OR EMAIL:

MONEY

MANIFESTED:	GRATEFULLY OUT:

TODAY I AM GRATEFUL FOR:

NOTES:

NEXT DAY GET AHEAD

DAILY LIFE MAGIC

DATE:

(S) (M) (T) (W) (T) (F) (S)

JOY LEVEL

TODAY'S INTENTIONS

REMINDER TO:

QUOTE FOR TODAY

INSPIRED THOUGHTS :

TODAY'S PRIORITIES:

EXERCISE:

TOTAL MINUTES:	
TOTAL STEPS:	

WATER INTAKE:

◊ ◊ ◊ ◊ ◊ ◊ ◊

MEAL TRACKER:

BREAKFAST:	LUNCH:
DINNER:	SNACKS:

TO CALL OR EMAIL:

MONEY

MANIFESTED:	GRATEFULLY OUT:

TODAY I AM GRATEFUL FOR:

NOTES:

NEXT DAY GET AHEAD

DAILY LIFE MAGIC

DATE:

(S) (M) (T) (W) (T) (F) (S)

JOY LEVEL

TODAY'S INTENTIONS

REMINDER TO:

QUOTE FOR TODAY

TODAY'S PRIORITES:

INSPIRED THOUGHTS:

EXERCISE:

TOTAL MINUTES:	
TOTAL STEPS:	

WATER INTAKE:

MEAL TRACKER:

BREAKFAST:	LUNCH:
DINNER:	SNACKS:

TO CALL OR EMAIL:

MONEY

MANIFESTED:	GRATEFULLY OUT:

TODAY I AM GRATEFUL FOR:

NOTES:

NEXT DAY GET AHEAD

DAILY LIFE MAGIC

DATE:
（S）（M）（T）（W）（T）（F）（S）

JOY LEVEL

TODAY'S INTENTIONS

REMINDER TO:

QUOTE FOR TODAY

TODAY'S PRIORITES:

INSPIRED THOUGHTS :

EXERCISE:

TOTAL MINUTES:	
TOTAL STEPS:	

WATER INTAKE:
○ ○ ○ ○ ○ ○ ○

MEAL TRACKER:

BREAKFAST:	LUNCH:
DINNER:	SNACKS:

TO CALL OR EMAIL:

MONEY

MANIFESTED:	GRATEFULLY OUT:

TODAY I AM GRATEFUL FOR:

NOTES:

NEXT DAY GET AHEAD

DAILY LIFE MAGIC

DATE:
(S) (M) (T) (W) (T) (F) (S)

JOY LEVEL

TODAY'S INTENTIONS

REMINDER TO:

QUOTE FOR TODAY

TODAY'S PRIORITES:

INSPIRED THOUGHTS:

EXERCISE:

TOTAL MINUTES:	
TOTAL STEPS:	

WATER INTAKE:

MEAL TRACKER:

BREAKFAST:	LUNCH:
DINNER:	SNACKS:

TO CALL OR EMAIL:

MONEY

MANIFESTED:	GRATEFULLY OUT:

TODAY I AM GRATEFUL FOR:

NOTES:

NEXT DAY GET AHEAD

DAILY LIFE MAGIC

DATE:

(S) (M) (T) (W) (T) (F) (S)

JOY LEVEL

TODAY'S INTENTIONS

REMINDER TO:

QUOTE FOR TODAY

INSPIRED THOUGHTS:

TODAY'S PRIORITES:

EXERCISE:

TOTAL MINUTES:	
TOTAL STEPS:	

WATER INTAKE:

MEAL TRACKER:

BREAKFAST:	LUNCH:
DINNER:	SNACKS:

TO CALL OR EMAIL:

MONEY

MANIFESTED:	GRATEFULLY OUT:

TODAY I AM GRATEFUL FOR:

NOTES:

NEXT DAY GET AHEAD

DAILY LIFE MAGIC

DATE:
(S) (M) (T) (W) (T) (F) (S)

JOY LEVEL

TODAY'S INTENTIONS

REMINDER TO:

QUOTE FOR TODAY

TODAY'S PRIORITES:

INSPIRED THOUGHTS:

EXERCISE:

TOTAL MINUTES:	
TOTAL STEPS:	

WATER INTAKE:

◊ ◊ ◊ ◊ ◊ ◊ ◊

MEAL TRACKER:

BREAKFAST:	LUNCH:
DINNER:	SNACKS:

TO CALL OR EMAIL:

MONEY

MANIFESTED:	GRATEFULLY OUT:

TODAY I AM GRATEFUL FOR:

NOTES:

NEXT DAY GET AHEAD

DAILY LIFE MAGIC

DATE:
(S) (T)   (S)

JOY LEVEL

TODAY'S INTENTIONS

REMINDER TO:

QUOTE FOR TODAY

INSPIRED THOUGHTS :

TODAY'S PRIORITES:

EXERCISE:

TOTAL MINUTES:	
TOTAL STEPS:	

WATER INTAKE:

◇ ◇ ◇ ◇ ◇ ◇ ◇

MEAL TRACKER:

BREAKFAST:	LUNCH:
DINNER:	SNACKS:

TO CALL OR EMAIL:

MONEY

MANIFESTED:	GRATEFULLY OUT:

TODAY I AM GRATEFUL FOR:

NOTES:

NEXT DAY GET AHEAD

DAILY LIFE MAGIC

DATE:

(S) (M) (T) (W) (T) (F) (S)

JOY LEVEL

TODAY'S INTENTIONS

REMINDER TO:

QUOTE FOR TODAY

INSPIRED THOUGHTS:

TODAY'S PRIORITES:

EXERCISE:

TOTAL MINUTES:	
TOTAL STEPS:	

WATER INTAKE:

MEAL TRACKER:

TO CALL OR EMAIL:

MONEY

BREAKFAST:	LUNCH:
DINNER:	SNACKS:

MANIFESTED:	GRATEFULLY OUT:

TODAY I AM GRATEFUL FOR:

NOTES:

NEXT DAY GET AHEAD

DAILY LIFE MAGIC

DATE:

Ⓢ Ⓜ Ⓣ Ⓦ Ⓣ Ⓕ Ⓢ

JOY LEVEL

TODAY'S INTENTIONS

REMINDER TO:

QUOTE FOR TODAY

TODAY'S PRIORITES:

INSPIRED THOUGHTS:

EXERCISE:

TOTAL MINUTES:	
TOTAL STEPS:	

WATER INTAKE:

○ ○ ○ ○ ○ ○ ○

MEAL TRACKER:

BREAKFAST:	LUNCH:
DINNER:	SNACKS:

TO CALL OR EMAIL:

MONEY

MANIFESTED:	GRATEFULLY OUT:

TODAY I AM GRATEFUL FOR:

NOTES:

NEXT DAY GET AHEAD

DAILY LIFE MAGIC

DATE:

S M T W T F S

JOY LEVEL

QUOTE FOR TODAY

TODAY'S INTENTIONS

REMINDER TO:

INSPIRED THOUGHTS :

TODAY'S PRIORITES:

EXERCISE:

TOTAL MINUTES:	
TOTAL STEPS:	

WATER INTAKE:

MEAL TRACKER:

BREAKFAST:	LUNCH:
DINNER:	SNACKS:

TO CALL OR EMAIL:

MONEY

MANIFESTED:	GRATEFULLY OUT:

TODAY I AM GRATEFUL FOR:

NOTES:

NEXT DAY GET AHEAD

DAILY LIFE MAGIC

DATE:
Ⓢ Ⓜ Ⓣ Ⓦ Ⓣ Ⓕ Ⓢ

JOY LEVEL

TODAY'S INTENTIONS

REMINDER TO:

QUOTE FOR TODAY

INSPIRED THOUGHTS :

TODAY'S PRIORITES:

EXERCISE:

TOTAL MINUTES:	
TOTAL STEPS:	

WATER INTAKE:

MEAL TRACKER:

BREAKFAST:	LUNCH:
DINNER:	SNACKS:

TO CALL OR EMAIL:

MONEY

MANIFESTED:	GRATEFULLY OUT:

TODAY I AM GRATEFUL FOR:

NOTES:

NEXT DAY GET AHEAD

DAILY LIFE MAGIC

DATE:
Ⓢ Ⓜ Ⓣ Ⓦ Ⓣ Ⓕ Ⓢ

JOY LEVEL

TODAY'S INTENTIONS

REMINDER TO:

QUOTE FOR TODAY

TODAY'S PRIORITES:

INSPIRED THOUGHTS :

EXERCISE:

TOTAL MINUTES:	
TOTAL STEPS:	

WATER INTAKE:

◊ ◊ ◊ ◊ ◊ ◊ ◊

MEAL TRACKER:

BREAKFAST:	LUNCH:
DINNER:	SNACKS:

TO CALL OR EMAIL:

MONEY

MANIFESTED:	GRATEFULLY OUT:

TODAY I AM GRATEFUL FOR:

NOTES:

NEXT DAY GET AHEAD

DAILY LIFE MAGIC

DATE:
Ⓢ Ⓜ Ⓣ Ⓦ Ⓣ Ⓕ Ⓢ

JOY LEVEL

TODAY'S INTENTIONS

REMINDER TO:

QUOTE FOR TODAY

INSPIRED THOUGHTS:

TODAY'S PRIORITIES:

EXERCISE:

TOTAL MINUTES:	
TOTAL STEPS:	

WATER INTAKE:
💧💧💧💧💧💧💧

MEAL TRACKER:

BREAKFAST:	LUNCH:
DINNER:	SNACKS:

TO CALL OR EMAIL:

MONEY

MANIFESTED:	GRATEFULLY OUT:

TODAY I AM GRATEFUL FOR:

NOTES:

NEXT DAY GET AHEAD

DAILY LIFE MAGIC

DATE:
(S) (M) (T) (W) (T) (F) (S)

JOY LEVEL

QUOTE FOR TODAY

TODAY'S INTENTIONS

REMINDER TO:

INSPIRED THOUGHTS:

TODAY'S PRIORITES:

EXERCISE:

TOTAL MINUTES:	
TOTAL STEPS:	

WATER INTAKE:

MEAL TRACKER:

BREAKFAST:	LUNCH:
DINNER:	SNACKS:

TO CALL OR EMAIL:

MONEY

MANIFESTED:	GRATEFULLY OUT:

TODAY I AM GRATEFUL FOR:

NOTES:

NEXT DAY GET AHEAD

DAILY LIFE MAGIC

DATE:
(S) (M) (T) (W) (T) (F) (S)

JOY LEVEL

TODAY'S INTENTIONS

REMINDER TO:

QUOTE FOR TODAY

INSPIRED THOUGHTS:

TODAY'S PRIORITES:

EXERCISE:

TOTAL MINUTES:	
TOTAL STEPS:	

WATER INTAKE:

MEAL TRACKER:

BREAKFAST:	LUNCH:
DINNER:	SNACKS:

TO CALL OR EMAIL:

MONEY

MANIFESTED:	GRATEFULLY OUT:

TODAY I AM GRATEFUL FOR:

NOTES:

NEXT DAY GET AHEAD

DAILY LIFE MAGIC

DATE:

(S) (M) (T) (W) (T) (F) (S)

JOY LEVEL

TODAY'S INTENTIONS

REMINDER TO:

QUOTE FOR TODAY

TODAY'S PRIORITES:

INSPIRED THOUGHTS :

EXERCISE:

TOTAL MINUTES:	
TOTAL STEPS:	

WATER INTAKE:

MEAL TRACKER:

BREAKFAST:	LUNCH:
DINNER:	SNACKS:

TO CALL OR EMAIL:

MONEY

MANIFESTED:	GRATEFULLY OUT:

TODAY I AM GRATEFUL FOR:

NOTES:

NEXT DAY GET AHEAD

DAILY LIFE MAGIC

DATE:

JOY LEVEL

TODAY'S INTENTIONS

REMINDER TO:

QUOTE FOR TODAY

TODAY'S PRIORITES:

INSPIRED THOUGHTS :

EXERCISE:

TOTAL MINUTES:	
TOTAL STEPS:	

WATER INTAKE:

MEAL TRACKER:

BREAKFAST:	LUNCH:
DINNER:	SNACKS:

TO CALL OR EMAIL:

MONEY

MANIFESTED:	GRATEFULLY OUT:

TODAY I AM GRATEFUL FOR:

NOTES:

NEXT DAY GET AHEAD

DAILY LIFE MAGIC

DATE:

(S) (M) (T) (W) (T) (F) (S)

JOY LEVEL

TODAY'S INTENTIONS

REMINDER TO:

QUOTE FOR TODAY

TODAY'S PRIORITES:

INSPIRED THOUGHTS:

EXERCISE:

TOTAL MINUTES:	
TOTAL STEPS:	

WATER INTAKE:

○ ○ ○ ○ ○ ○ ○

MEAL TRACKER:

BREAKFAST:	LUNCH:
DINNER:	SNACKS:

TO CALL OR EMAIL:

MONEY

MANIFESTED:	GRATEFULLY OUT:

TODAY I AM GRATEFUL FOR:

NOTES:

NEXT DAY GET AHEAD

DAILY LIFE MAGIC

DATE:

Ⓢ Ⓜ Ⓣ Ⓦ Ⓣ Ⓕ Ⓢ

JOY LEVEL

TODAY'S INTENTIONS

REMINDER TO:

QUOTE FOR TODAY

INSPIRED THOUGHTS :

TODAY'S PRIORITIES:

EXERCISE:

TOTAL MINUTES:	
TOTAL STEPS:	

WATER INTAKE:

MEAL TRACKER:

BREAKFAST:	LUNCH:
DINNER:	SNACKS:

TO CALL OR EMAIL:

MONEY

MANIFESTED:	GRATEFULLY OUT:

TODAY I AM GRATEFUL FOR:

NOTES:

NEXT DAY GET AHEAD

DAILY LIFE MAGIC

DATE:

(S) (M) (T) (W) (T) (F) (S)

JOY LEVEL

TODAY'S INTENTIONS

REMINDER TO:

QUOTE FOR TODAY

INSPIRED THOUGHTS:

TODAY'S PRIORITES:

EXERCISE:

TOTAL MINUTES:	
TOTAL STEPS:	

WATER INTAKE:

○ ○ ○ ○ ○ ○ ○

MEAL TRACKER:

TO CALL OR EMAIL:

MONEY

BREAKFAST:	LUNCH:
DINNER:	SNACKS:

MANIFESTED:	GRATEFULLY OUT:

TODAY I AM GRATEFUL FOR:

NOTES:

NEXT DAY GET AHEAD

DAILY LIFE MAGIC

DATE:
(S) (M) (T) (W) (T) (F) (S)

JOY LEVEL

TODAY'S INTENTIONS

REMINDER TO:

QUOTE FOR TODAY

INSPIRED THOUGHTS:

TODAY'S PRIORITES:

EXERCISE:

TOTAL MINUTES:	
TOTAL STEPS:	

WATER INTAKE:

MEAL TRACKER:

BREAKFAST:	LUNCH:
DINNER:	SNACKS:

TO CALL OR EMAIL:

MONEY

MANIFESTED:	GRATEFULLY OUT:

TODAY I AM GRATEFUL FOR:

NOTES:

NEXT DAY GET AHEAD

DAILY LIFE MAGIC

DATE:

(S) (M) (T) (W) (T) (F) (S)

JOY LEVEL

😄 🙂 😐 🙁 😢

QUOTE FOR TODAY

TODAY'S INTENTIONS

REMINDER TO:

INSPIRED THOUGHTS :

TODAY'S PRIORITES:

EXERCISE:

TOTAL MINUTES:	
TOTAL STEPS:	

WATER INTAKE:

💧💧💧💧💧💧💧

MEAL TRACKER:

BREAKFAST:	LUNCH:
DINNER:	SNACKS:

TO CALL OR EMAIL:

MONEY

MANIFESTED:	GRATEFULLY OUT:

TODAY I AM GRATEFUL FOR:

NOTES:

NEXT DAY GET AHEAD

DAILY LIFE MAGIC

DATE:

(S) (M) (T) (W) (T) (F) (S)

JOY LEVEL

TODAY'S INTENTIONS

REMINDER TO:

QUOTE FOR TODAY

INSPIRED THOUGHTS:

TODAY'S PRIORITES:

EXERCISE:

TOTAL MINUTES:	
TOTAL STEPS:	

WATER INTAKE:

◊ ◊ ◊ ◊ ◊ ◊ ◊

MEAL TRACKER:

BREAKFAST:	LUNCH:
DINNER:	SNACKS:

TO CALL OR EMAIL:

MONEY

MANIFESTED:	GRATEFULLY OUT:

TODAY I AM GRATEFUL FOR:

NOTES:

NEXT DAY GET AHEAD

DAILY LIFE MAGIC

DATE:
Ⓢ Ⓜ Ⓣ Ⓦ Ⓣ Ⓕ Ⓢ

JOY LEVEL

😃 🙂 😐 🙁 😢

QUOTE FOR TODAY

TODAY'S INTENTIONS

REMINDER TO:

TODAY'S PRIORITES:

INSPIRED THOUGHTS :

EXERCISE:

TOTAL MINUTES:	
TOTAL STEPS:	

WATER INTAKE:

💧 💧 💧 💧 💧 💧 💧

MEAL TRACKER:

BREAKFAST:	LUNCH:
DINNER:	SNACKS:

TO CALL OR EMAIL:

MONEY

MANIFESTED:	GRATEFULLY OUT:

TODAY I AM GRATEFUL FOR:

NOTES:

NEXT DAY GET AHEAD

DAILY LIFE MAGIC

DATE:

Ⓢ Ⓜ Ⓣ Ⓦ Ⓣ Ⓕ Ⓢ

JOY LEVEL

TODAY'S INTENTIONS

REMINDER TO:

QUOTE FOR TODAY

INSPIRED THOUGHTS:

TODAY'S PRIORITES:

EXERCISE:

TOTAL MINUTES:	
TOTAL STEPS:	

WATER INTAKE:

💧💧💧💧💧💧💧

MEAL TRACKER:

BREAKFAST:	LUNCH:
DINNER:	SNACKS:

TO CALL OR EMAIL:

MONEY

MANIFESTED:	GRATEFULLY OUT:

TODAY I AM GRATEFUL FOR:

NOTES:

NEXT DAY GET AHEAD

DAILY LIFE MAGIC

DATE:
(S) (M) (T) (W) (T) (F) (S)

JOY LEVEL

QUOTE FOR TODAY

TODAY'S INTENTIONS

REMINDER TO:

INSPIRED THOUGHTS:

TODAY'S PRIORITES:

EXERCISE:

TOTAL MINUTES:	
TOTAL STEPS:	

WATER INTAKE:

MEAL TRACKER:

BREAKFAST:	LUNCH:
DINNER:	SNACKS:

TO CALL OR EMAIL:

MONEY

MANIFESTED:	GRATEFULLY OUT:

TODAY I AM GRATEFUL FOR:

NOTES:

NEXT DAY GET AHEAD

DAILY LIFE MAGIC

DATE:

S M T W T F S

JOY LEVEL

😃 🙂 😐 🙁 😢

QUOTE FOR TODAY

TODAY'S INTENTIONS

REMINDER TO:

TODAY'S PRIORITES:

EXERCISE:

TOTAL MINUTES:	
TOTAL STEPS:	

WATER INTAKE:

💧 💧 💧 💧 💧 💧 💧

MEAL TRACKER:

BREAKFAST:	LUNCH:
DINNER:	SNACKS:

TO CALL OR EMAIL:

INSPIRED THOUGHTS :

MONEY

MANIFESTED:	GRATEFULLY OUT:

TODAY I AM GRATEFUL FOR:

NOTES:

NEXT DAY GET AHEAD

DAILY LIFE MAGIC

DATE:

(S) (M) (T) (W) (T) (F) (S)

JOY LEVEL

TODAY'S INTENTIONS

REMINDER TO:

QUOTE FOR TODAY

TODAY'S PRIORITES:

INSPIRED THOUGHTS:

EXERCISE:

TOTAL MINUTES:	
TOTAL STEPS:	

WATER INTAKE:

MEAL TRACKER:

BREAKFAST:	LUNCH:
DINNER:	SNACKS:

TO CALL OR EMAIL:

MONEY

MANIFESTED:	GRATEFULLY OUT:

TODAY I AM GRATEFUL FOR:

NOTES:

NEXT DAY GET AHEAD

DAILY LIFE MAGIC

DATE:

S M T W T F S

JOY LEVEL

TODAY'S INTENTIONS

REMINDER TO:

QUOTE FOR TODAY

INSPIRED THOUGHTS :

TODAY'S PRIORITES:

EXERCISE:

TOTAL MINUTES:	
TOTAL STEPS:	

WATER INTAKE:

MEAL TRACKER:

BREAKFAST:	LUNCH:
DINNER:	SNACKS:

TO CALL OR EMAIL:

MONEY

MANIFESTED:	GRATEFULLY OUT:

TODAY I AM GRATEFUL FOR:

NOTES:

NEXT DAY GET AHEAD

DAILY LIFE MAGIC

DATE:

(S) (M) (T) (W) (T) (F) (S)

JOY LEVEL

TODAY'S INTENTIONS

REMINDER TO:

QUOTE FOR TODAY

TODAY'S PRIORITES:

INSPIRED THOUGHTS:

EXERCISE:

TOTAL MINUTES:	
TOTAL STEPS:	

WATER INTAKE:

MEAL TRACKER:

BREAKFAST:	LUNCH:
DINNER:	SNACKS:

TO CALL OR EMAIL:

MONEY

MANIFESTED:	GRATEFULLY OUT:

TODAY I AM GRATEFUL FOR:

NOTES:

NEXT DAY GET AHEAD

DAILY LIFE MAGIC

DATE:

JOY LEVEL

TODAY'S INTENTIONS

REMINDER TO:

QUOTE FOR TODAY

INSPIRED THOUGHTS :

TODAY'S PRIORITES:

EXERCISE:

TOTAL MINUTES:	
TOTAL STEPS:	

WATER INTAKE:

◊ ◊ ◊ ◊ ◊ ◊ ◊

MEAL TRACKER:

BREAKFAST:	LUNCH:
DINNER:	SNACKS:

TO CALL OR EMAIL:

MONEY

MANIFESTED:	GRATEFULLY OUT:

TODAY I AM GRATEFUL FOR:

NOTES:

NEXT DAY GET AHEAD

DAILY LIFE MAGIC

DATE:

(S) (M) (T) (W) (T) (F) (S)

JOY LEVEL

TODAY'S INTENTIONS

REMINDER TO:

QUOTE FOR TODAY

INSPIRED THOUGHTS:

TODAY'S PRIORITES:

EXERCISE:

TOTAL MINUTES:	
TOTAL STEPS:	

WATER INTAKE:

MEAL TRACKER:

BREAKFAST:	LUNCH:
DINNER:	SNACKS:

TO CALL OR EMAIL:

MONEY

MANIFESTED:	GRATEFULLY OUT:

TODAY I AM GRATEFUL FOR:

NOTES:

NEXT DAY GET AHEAD

DAILY LIFE MAGIC

DATE:
Ⓢ Ⓜ Ⓣ Ⓦ Ⓣ Ⓕ Ⓢ

JOY LEVEL

TODAY'S INTENTIONS

REMINDER TO:

QUOTE FOR TODAY

INSPIRED THOUGHTS :

TODAY'S PRIORITES:

EXERCISE:

TOTAL MINUTES:	
TOTAL STEPS:	

WATER INTAKE:
💧💧💧💧💧💧💧

MEAL TRACKER:

BREAKFAST:	LUNCH:
DINNER:	SNACKS:

TO CALL OR EMAIL:

MONEY

MANIFESTED:	GRATEFULLY OUT:

TODAY I AM GRATEFUL FOR:

NOTES:

NEXT DAY GET AHEAD

DAILY LIFE MAGIC

DATE:

Ⓢ Ⓜ Ⓣ Ⓦ Ⓣ Ⓕ Ⓢ

JOY LEVEL

😄 🙂 😐 🙁 😢

QUOTE FOR TODAY

TODAY'S INTENTIONS

REMINDER TO:

INSPIRED THOUGHTS:

TODAY'S PRIORITES:

EXERCISE:

TOTAL MINUTES:	
TOTAL STEPS:	

WATER INTAKE:

💧 💧 💧 💧 💧 💧 💧

MEAL TRACKER:

BREAKFAST:	LUNCH:
DINNER:	SNACKS:

TO CALL OR EMAIL:

MONEY

MANIFESTED:	GRATEFULLY OUT:

TODAY I AM GRATEFUL FOR:

NOTES:

NEXT DAY GET AHEAD

DAILY LIFE MAGIC

DATE:

JOY LEVEL

TODAY'S INTENTIONS

REMINDER TO:

QUOTE FOR TODAY

INSPIRED THOUGHTS :

TODAY'S PRIORITES:

EXERCISE:

TOTAL MINUTES:	
TOTAL STEPS:	

WATER INTAKE:

MEAL TRACKER:

BREAKFAST:	LUNCH:
DINNER:	SNACKS:

TO CALL OR EMAIL:

MONEY

MANIFESTED:	GRATEFULLY OUT:

TODAY I AM GRATEFUL FOR:

NOTES:

NEXT DAY GET AHEAD

DAILY LIFE MAGIC

DATE:
Ⓢ Ⓜ Ⓣ Ⓦ Ⓣ Ⓕ Ⓢ

JOY LEVEL

TODAY'S INTENTIONS

REMINDER TO:

QUOTE FOR TODAY

INSPIRED THOUGHTS :

TODAY'S PRIORITES:

EXERCISE:

TOTAL MINUTES:	
TOTAL STEPS:	

WATER INTAKE:

◯ ◯ ◯ ◯ ◯ ◯ ◯

MEAL TRACKER:

BREAKFAST:	LUNCH:
DINNER:	SNACKS:

TO CALL OR EMAIL:

MONEY

MANIFESTED:	GRATEFULLY OUT:

TODAY I AM GRATEFUL FOR:

NOTES:

NEXT DAY GET AHEAD

DAILY LIFE MAGIC

DATE:

(S) (M) (T) (W) (T) (F) (S)

JOY LEVEL

TODAY'S INTENTIONS

REMINDER TO:

QUOTE FOR TODAY

INSPIRED THOUGHTS :

TODAY'S PRIORITES:

EXERCISE:

TOTAL MINUTES:	
TOTAL STEPS:	

WATER INTAKE:

MEAL TRACKER:

BREAKFAST:	LUNCH:
DINNER:	SNACKS:

TO CALL OR EMAIL:

MONEY

MANIFESTED:	GRATEFULLY OUT:

TODAY I AM GRATEFUL FOR:

NOTES:

NEXT DAY GET AHEAD

DAILY LIFE MAGIC

DATE:

(S) (M) (T) (W) (T) (F) (S)

JOY LEVEL

TODAY'S INTENTIONS

REMINDER TO:

QUOTE FOR TODAY

INSPIRED THOUGHTS:

TODAY'S PRIORITES:

EXERCISE:

TOTAL MINUTES:	
TOTAL STEPS:	

WATER INTAKE:

MEAL TRACKER:

BREAKFAST:	LUNCH:
DINNER:	SNACKS:

TO CALL OR EMAIL:

MONEY

MANIFESTED:	GRATEFULLY OUT:

TODAY I AM GRATEFUL FOR:

NOTES:

NEXT DAY GET AHEAD

DAILY LIFE MAGIC

DATE:
Ⓢ Ⓜ Ⓣ Ⓦ Ⓣ Ⓕ Ⓢ

JOY LEVEL

TODAY'S INTENTIONS

REMINDER TO:

QUOTE FOR TODAY

INSPIRED THOUGHTS :

TODAY'S PRIORITES:

EXERCISE:

TOTAL MINUTES:	
TOTAL STEPS:	

WATER INTAKE:
◌ ◌ ◌ ◌ ◌ ◌ ◌

MEAL TRACKER:

TO CALL OR EMAIL:

MONEY

BREAKFAST:	LUNCH:
DINNER:	SNACKS:

MANIFESTED:	GRATEFULLY OUT:

TODAY I AM GRATEFUL FOR:

NOTES:

NEXT DAY GET AHEAD

DAILY LIFE MAGIC

DATE:
(S) (M) (T) (W) (T) (F) (S)

JOY LEVEL

TODAY'S INTENTIONS

REMINDER TO:

QUOTE FOR TODAY

TODAY'S PRIORITES:

INSPIRED THOUGHTS :

EXERCISE:

TOTAL MINUTES:	
TOTAL STEPS:	

WATER INTAKE:

MEAL TRACKER:

BREAKFAST:	LUNCH:
DINNER:	SNACKS:

TO CALL OR EMAIL:

MONEY

MANIFESTED:	GRATEFULLY OUT:

TODAY I AM GRATEFUL FOR:

NOTES:

NEXT DAY GET AHEAD

DAILY LIFE MAGIC

DATE:

JOY LEVEL

TODAY'S INTENTIONS

REMINDER TO:

QUOTE FOR TODAY

INSPIRED THOUGHTS :

TODAY'S PRIORITES:

EXERCISE:

TOTAL MINUTES:	
TOTAL STEPS:	

WATER INTAKE:

MEAL TRACKER:

TO CALL OR EMAIL:

MONEY

BREAKFAST:	LUNCH:
DINNER:	SNACKS:

MANIFESTED:	GRATEFULLY OUT:

TODAY I AM GRATEFUL FOR:

NOTES:

NEXT DAY GET AHEAD

DAILY LIFE MAGIC

DATE:

(S) (M) (T) (W) (T) (F) (S)

JOY LEVEL

TODAY'S INTENTIONS

REMINDER TO:

QUOTE FOR TODAY

TODAY'S PRIORITES:

INSPIRED THOUGHTS:

EXERCISE:

TOTAL MINUTES:	
TOTAL STEPS:	

WATER INTAKE:

MEAL TRACKER:

BREAKFAST:	LUNCH:
DINNER:	SNACKS:

TO CALL OR EMAIL:

MONEY

MANIFESTED:	GRATEFULLY OUT:

TODAY I AM GRATEFUL FOR:

NOTES:

NEXT DAY GET AHEAD

DAILY LIFE MAGIC

DATE:

JOY LEVEL

TODAY'S INTENTIONS

REMINDER TO:

QUOTE FOR TODAY

INSPIRED THOUGHTS:

TODAY'S PRIORITES:

EXERCISE:

TOTAL MINUTES:	
TOTAL STEPS:	

WATER INTAKE:

MEAL TRACKER:

BREAKFAST:	LUNCH:
DINNER:	SNACKS:

TO CALL OR EMAIL:

MONEY

MANIFESTED:	GRATEFULLY OUT:

TODAY I AM GRATEFUL FOR:

NOTES:

NEXT DAY GET AHEAD

DAILY LIFE MAGIC

DATE:
(S) (M) (T) (W) (T) (F) (S)

JOY LEVEL

TODAY'S INTENTIONS

REMINDER TO:

QUOTE FOR TODAY

INSPIRED THOUGHTS:

TODAY'S PRIORITIES:

EXERCISE:

TOTAL MINUTES:	
TOTAL STEPS:	

WATER INTAKE:

MEAL TRACKER:

TO CALL OR EMAIL:

MONEY

BREAKFAST:	LUNCH:
DINNER:	SNACKS:

MANIFESTED:	GRATEFULLY OUT:

TODAY I AM GRATEFUL FOR:

NOTES:

NEXT DAY GET AHEAD

DAILY LIFE MAGIC

DATE:

JOY LEVEL

TODAY'S INTENTIONS

REMINDER TO:

QUOTE FOR TODAY

INSPIRED THOUGHTS:

TODAY'S PRIORITES:

EXERCISE:

TOTAL MINUTES:	
TOTAL STEPS:	

WATER INTAKE:

◊ ◊ ◊ ◊ ◊ ◊ ◊

MEAL TRACKER:

BREAKFAST:	LUNCH:
DINNER:	SNACKS:

TO CALL OR EMAIL:

MONEY

MANIFESTED:	GRATEFULLY OUT:

TODAY I AM GRATEFUL FOR:

NOTES:

NEXT DAY GET AHEAD

DAILY LIFE MAGIC

DATE:

Ⓢ Ⓜ Ⓣ Ⓦ Ⓣ Ⓕ Ⓢ

JOY LEVEL

😄 🙂 😐 🙁 😢

QUOTE FOR TODAY

TODAY'S INTENTIONS

REMINDER TO:

INSPIRED THOUGHTS:

TODAY'S PRIORITIES:

EXERCISE:

TOTAL MINUTES:	
TOTAL STEPS:	

WATER INTAKE:

💧 💧 💧 💧 💧 💧 💧

MEAL TRACKER:

BREAKFAST:	LUNCH:
DINNER:	SNACKS:

TO CALL OR EMAIL:

MONEY

MANIFESTED:	GRATEFULLY OUT:

TODAY I AM GRATEFUL FOR:

NOTES:

NEXT DAY GET AHEAD

DAILY LIFE MAGIC

DATE:
Ⓢ Ⓜ Ⓣ Ⓦ Ⓣ Ⓕ Ⓢ

JOY LEVEL

TODAY'S INTENTIONS

REMINDER TO:

QUOTE FOR TODAY

INSPIRED THOUGHTS:

TODAY'S PRIORITES:

EXERCISE:

TOTAL MINUTES:	
TOTAL STEPS:	

WATER INTAKE:
○ ○ ○ ○ ○ ○ ○

MEAL TRACKER:

BREAKFAST:	LUNCH:
DINNER:	SNACKS:

TO CALL OR EMAIL:

MONEY

MANIFESTED:	GRATEFULLY OUT:

TODAY I AM GRATEFUL FOR:

NOTES:

NEXT DAY GET AHEAD

DAILY LIFE MAGIC

DATE:

Ⓢ Ⓜ Ⓣ Ⓦ Ⓣ Ⓕ Ⓢ

JOY LEVEL

😊 🙂 😐 🙁 😢

TODAY'S INTENTIONS

REMINDER TO:

QUOTE FOR TODAY

TODAY'S PRIORITES:

INSPIRED THOUGHTS:

EXERCISE:

TOTAL MINUTES:	
TOTAL STEPS:	

WATER INTAKE:

💧 💧 💧 💧 💧 💧 💧

MEAL TRACKER:

BREAKFAST:	LUNCH:
DINNER:	SNACKS:

TO CALL OR EMAIL:

MONEY

MANIFESTED:	GRATEFULLY OUT:

TODAY I AM GRATEFUL FOR:

NOTES:

NEXT DAY GET AHEAD

DAILY LIFE MAGIC

DATE:

JOY LEVEL

TODAY'S INTENTIONS

REMINDER TO:

QUOTE FOR TODAY

INSPIRED THOUGHTS :

TODAY'S PRIORITES:

EXERCISE:

TOTAL MINUTES:	
TOTAL STEPS:	

WATER INTAKE:

MEAL TRACKER:

BREAKFAST:	LUNCH:
DINNER:	SNACKS:

TO CALL OR EMAIL:

MONEY

MANIFESTED:	GRATEFULLY OUT:

TODAY I AM GRATEFUL FOR:

NOTES:

NEXT DAY GET AHEAD

DAILY LIFE MAGIC

DATE:
(S) (M) (T) (W) (T) (F) (S)

JOY LEVEL

TODAY'S INTENTIONS

REMINDER TO:

QUOTE FOR TODAY

TODAY'S PRIORITES:

INSPIRED THOUGHTS :

EXERCISE:

TOTAL MINUTES:	
TOTAL STEPS:	

WATER INTAKE:

MEAL TRACKER:

BREAKFAST:	LUNCH:
DINNER:	SNACKS:

TO CALL OR EMAIL:

MONEY

MANIFESTED:	GRATEFULLY OUT:

TODAY I AM GRATEFUL FOR:

NOTES:

NEXT DAY GET AHEAD

DAILY LIFE MAGIC

DATE:

(S) (M) (T) (W) (T) (F) (S)

JOY LEVEL

TODAY'S INTENTIONS

REMINDER TO:

QUOTE FOR TODAY

INSPIRED THOUGHTS :

TODAY'S PRIORITES:

EXERCISE:

TOTAL MINUTES:	
TOTAL STEPS:	

WATER INTAKE:

◊ ◊ ◊ ◊ ◊ ◊

MEAL TRACKER:

BREAKFAST:	LUNCH:
DINNER:	SNACKS:

TO CALL OR EMAIL:

MONEY

MANIFESTED:	GRATEFULLY OUT:

TODAY I AM GRATEFUL FOR:

NOTES:

NEXT DAY GET AHEAD

DAILY LIFE MAGIC

DATE:

Ⓢ Ⓜ Ⓣ Ⓦ Ⓣ Ⓕ Ⓢ

JOY LEVEL

TODAY'S INTENTIONS

REMINDER TO:

QUOTE FOR TODAY

INSPIRED THOUGHTS:

TODAY'S PRIORITES:

EXERCISE:

TOTAL MINUTES:	
TOTAL STEPS:	

WATER INTAKE:

💧 💧 💧 💧 💧 💧 💧

MEAL TRACKER:

BREAKFAST:	LUNCH:
DINNER:	SNACKS:

TO CALL OR EMAIL:

MONEY

MANIFESTED:	GRATEFULLY OUT:

TODAY I AM GRATEFUL FOR:

NOTES:

NEXT DAY GET AHEAD

DAILY LIFE MAGIC

DATE:
(S) (M) (T) (W) (T) (F) (S)

JOY LEVEL

TODAY'S INTENTIONS

REMINDER TO:

QUOTE FOR TODAY

INSPIRED THOUGHTS:

TODAY'S PRIORITES:

EXERCISE:

TOTAL MINUTES:	
TOTAL STEPS:	

WATER INTAKE:
◯ ◯ ◯ ◯ ◯ ◯ ◯

MEAL TRACKER:

BREAKFAST:	LUNCH:
DINNER:	SNACKS:

TO CALL OR EMAIL:

MONEY

MANIFESTED:	GRATEFULLY OUT:

TODAY I AM GRATEFUL FOR:

NOTES:

NEXT DAY GET AHEAD

DAILY LIFE MAGIC

DATE:
(S) (M) (T) (W) (T) (F) (S)

JOY LEVEL

TODAY'S INTENTIONS

REMINDER TO:

QUOTE FOR TODAY

INSPIRED THOUGHTS:

TODAY'S PRIORITES:

EXERCISE:

TOTAL MINUTES:	
TOTAL STEPS:	

WATER INTAKE:

MEAL TRACKER:

BREAKFAST:	LUNCH:
DINNER:	SNACKS:

TO CALL OR EMAIL:

MONEY

MANIFESTED:	GRATEFULLY OUT:

TODAY I AM GRATEFUL FOR:

NOTES:

NEXT DAY GET AHEAD

DAILY LIFE MAGIC

DATE:

Ⓢ Ⓜ Ⓣ Ⓦ Ⓣ Ⓕ Ⓢ

JOY LEVEL

TODAY'S INTENTIONS

REMINDER TO:

QUOTE FOR TODAY

INSPIRED THOUGHTS :

TODAY'S PRIORITIES:

EXERCISE:

TOTAL MINUTES:	
TOTAL STEPS:	

WATER INTAKE:

💧 💧 💧 💧 💧 💧 💧

MEAL TRACKER:

TO CALL OR EMAIL:

MONEY

BREAKFAST:	LUNCH:
DINNER:	SNACKS:

MANIFESTED:	GRATEFULLY OUT:

TODAY I AM GRATEFUL FOR:

NOTES:

NEXT DAY GET AHEAD

DAILY LIFE MAGIC

DATE:

(S) (M) (T) (W) (T) (F) (S)

JOY LEVEL

TODAY'S INTENTIONS

REMINDER TO:

QUOTE FOR TODAY

INSPIRED THOUGHTS:

TODAY'S PRIORITES:

EXERCISE:

TOTAL MINUTES:	
TOTAL STEPS:	

WATER INTAKE:

MEAL TRACKER:

BREAKFAST:	LUNCH:
DINNER:	SNACKS:

TO CALL OR EMAIL:

MONEY

MANIFESTED:	GRATEFULLY OUT:

TODAY I AM GRATEFUL FOR:

NOTES:

NEXT DAY GET AHEAD

DAILY LIFE MAGIC

DATE:

JOY LEVEL

TODAY'S INTENTIONS

REMINDER TO:

QUOTE FOR TODAY

INSPIRED THOUGHTS :

TODAY'S PRIORITES:

EXERCISE:

TOTAL MINUTES:	
TOTAL STEPS:	

WATER INTAKE:
◊ ◊ ◊ ◊ ◊ ◊

MEAL TRACKER:

BREAKFAST:	LUNCH:
DINNER:	SNACKS:

TO CALL OR EMAIL:

MONEY

MANIFESTED:	GRATEFULLY OUT:

TODAY I AM GRATEFUL FOR:

NOTES:

NEXT DAY GET AHEAD

DAILY LIFE MAGIC

DATE:
Ⓢ Ⓜ Ⓣ Ⓦ Ⓣ Ⓕ Ⓢ

JOY LEVEL

😄 🙂 😐 🙁 😢

QUOTE FOR TODAY

TODAY'S INTENTIONS

REMINDER TO:

INSPIRED THOUGHTS:

EXERCISE:

TOTAL MINUTES:	
TOTAL STEPS:	

TODAY'S PRIORITIES:

WATER INTAKE:

💧 💧 💧 💧 💧 💧 💧

MEAL TRACKER:

BREAKFAST:	LUNCH:
DINNER:	SNACKS:

TO CALL OR EMAIL:

MONEY

MANIFESTED:	GRATEFULLY OUT:

TODAY I AM GRATEFUL FOR:

NOTES:

NEXT DAY GET AHEAD

DAILY LIFE MAGIC

DATE:

JOY LEVEL

TODAY'S INTENTIONS

REMINDER TO:

QUOTE FOR TODAY

INSPIRED THOUGHTS :

TODAY'S PRIORITES:

EXERCISE:

TOTAL MINUTES:	
TOTAL STEPS:	

WATER INTAKE:

MEAL TRACKER:

BREAKFAST:	LUNCH:
DINNER:	SNACKS:

TO CALL OR EMAIL:

MONEY

MANIFESTED:	GRATEFULLY OUT:

TODAY I AM GRATEFUL FOR:

NOTES:

NEXT DAY GET AHEAD

DAILY LIFE MAGIC

DATE:

(S) (M) (T) (W) (T) (F) (S)

JOY LEVEL

TODAY'S INTENTIONS

REMINDER TO:

QUOTE FOR TODAY

INSPIRED THOUGHTS :

TODAY'S PRIORITES:

EXERCISE:

TOTAL MINUTES:	
TOTAL STEPS:	

WATER INTAKE:

MEAL TRACKER:

BREAKFAST:	LUNCH:
DINNER:	SNACKS:

TO CALL OR EMAIL:

MONEY

MANIFESTED:	GRATEFULLY OUT:

TODAY I AM GRATEFUL FOR:

NOTES:

NEXT DAY GET AHEAD

DAILY LIFE MAGIC

DATE:
Ⓢ Ⓜ Ⓣ Ⓦ Ⓣ Ⓕ Ⓢ

JOY LEVEL

TODAY'S INTENTIONS

REMINDER TO:

QUOTE FOR TODAY

INSPIRED THOUGHTS :

TODAY'S PRIORITES:

EXERCISE:

TOTAL MINUTES:	
TOTAL STEPS:	

WATER INTAKE:

MEAL TRACKER:

BREAKFAST:	LUNCH:
DINNER:	SNACKS:

TO CALL OR EMAIL:

MONEY

MANIFESTED:	GRATEFULLY OUT:

TODAY I AM GRATEFUL FOR:

NOTES:

NEXT DAY GET AHEAD

DAILY LIFE MAGIC

DATE:
(S) (M) (T) (W) (T) (F) (S)

JOY LEVEL

TODAY'S INTENTIONS

REMINDER TO:

QUOTE FOR TODAY

INSPIRED THOUGHTS:

TODAY'S PRIORITIES:

EXERCISE:

TOTAL MINUTES:	
TOTAL STEPS:	

WATER INTAKE:

MEAL TRACKER:

BREAKFAST:	LUNCH:
DINNER:	SNACKS:

TO CALL OR EMAIL:

MONEY

MANIFESTED:	GRATEFULLY OUT:

TODAY I AM GRATEFUL FOR:

NOTES:

NEXT DAY GET AHEAD

DAILY LIFE MAGIC

DATE:
Ⓢ Ⓜ Ⓣ Ⓦ Ⓣ Ⓕ Ⓢ

JOY LEVEL

TODAY'S INTENTIONS

REMINDER TO:

QUOTE FOR TODAY

INSPIRED THOUGHTS:

TODAY'S PRIORITES:

EXERCISE:

TOTAL MINUTES:	
TOTAL STEPS:	

WATER INTAKE:
○ ○ ○ ○ ○ ○ ○

MEAL TRACKER:

BREAKFAST:	LUNCH:
DINNER:	SNACKS:

TO CALL OR EMAIL:

MONEY

MANIFESTED:	GRATEFULLY OUT:

TODAY I AM GRATEFUL FOR:

NOTES:

NEXT DAY GET AHEAD

DAILY LIFE MAGIC

DATE:

Ⓢ Ⓜ Ⓣ Ⓦ Ⓣ Ⓕ Ⓢ

JOY LEVEL

TODAY'S INTENTIONS

REMINDER TO:

QUOTE FOR TODAY

INSPIRED THOUGHTS:

TODAY'S PRIORITES:

EXERCISE:

TOTAL MINUTES:	
TOTAL STEPS:	

WATER INTAKE:

◯ ◯ ◯ ◯ ◯ ◯ ◯

MEAL TRACKER:

TO CALL OR EMAIL:

MONEY

BREAKFAST:	LUNCH:
DINNER:	SNACKS:

MANIFESTED:	GRATEFULLY OUT:

TODAY I AM GRATEFUL FOR:

NOTES:

NEXT DAY GET AHEAD

DAILY LIFE MAGIC

DATE:

(S) (M) (T) (W) (T) (F) (S)

JOY LEVEL

TODAY'S INTENTIONS

REMINDER TO:

QUOTE FOR TODAY

INSPIRED THOUGHTS :

TODAY'S PRIORITES:

EXERCISE:

TOTAL MINUTES:	
TOTAL STEPS:	

WATER INTAKE:

◯ ◯ ◯ ◯ ◯ ◯ ◯

MEAL TRACKER:

BREAKFAST:	LUNCH:
DINNER:	SNACKS:

TO CALL OR EMAIL:

MONEY

MANIFESTED:	GRATEFULLY OUT:

TODAY I AM GRATEFUL FOR:

NOTES:

NEXT DAY GET AHEAD

DAILY LIFE MAGIC

DATE:

(S) (M) (T) (W) (T) (F) (S)

JOY LEVEL

TODAY'S INTENTIONS

REMINDER TO:

QUOTE FOR TODAY

INSPIRED THOUGHTS :

TODAY'S PRIORITES:

EXERCISE:

TOTAL MINUTES:	
TOTAL STEPS:	

WATER INTAKE:

◊ ◊ ◊ ◊ ◊ ◊ ◊

MEAL TRACKER:

BREAKFAST:	LUNCH:
DINNER:	SNACKS:

TO CALL OR EMAIL:

MONEY

MANIFESTED:	GRATEFULLY OUT:

TODAY I AM GRATEFUL FOR:

NOTES:

NEXT DAY GET AHEAD

DAILY LIFE MAGIC

DATE:

S M T W T F S

JOY LEVEL

QUOTE FOR TODAY

TODAY'S INTENTIONS

REMINDER TO:

INSPIRED THOUGHTS :

TODAY'S PRIORITES:

EXERCISE:

TOTAL MINUTES:	
TOTAL STEPS:	

WATER INTAKE:

MEAL TRACKER:

BREAKFAST:	LUNCH:
DINNER:	SNACKS:

TO CALL OR EMAIL:

MONEY

MANIFESTED:	GRATEFULLY OUT:

TODAY I AM GRATEFUL FOR:

NOTES:

NEXT DAY GET AHEAD

DAILY LIFE MAGIC

DATE:

(S) (M) (T) (W) (T) (F) (S)

JOY LEVEL

TODAY'S INTENTIONS

REMINDER TO:

QUOTE FOR TODAY

INSPIRED THOUGHTS:

TODAY'S PRIORITES:

EXERCISE:

TOTAL MINUTES:	
TOTAL STEPS:	

WATER INTAKE:

MEAL TRACKER:

BREAKFAST:	LUNCH:
DINNER:	SNACKS:

TO CALL OR EMAIL:

MONEY

MANIFESTED:	GRATEFULLY OUT:

TODAY I AM GRATEFUL FOR:

NOTES:

NEXT DAY GET AHEAD

DAILY LIFE MAGIC

DATE:

JOY LEVEL

TODAY'S INTENTIONS

REMINDER TO:

QUOTE FOR TODAY

INSPIRED THOUGHTS :

TODAY'S PRIORITES:

EXERCISE:

TOTAL MINUTES:	
TOTAL STEPS:	

WATER INTAKE:

MEAL TRACKER:

BREAKFAST:	LUNCH:
DINNER:	SNACKS:

TO CALL OR EMAIL:

MONEY

MANIFESTED:	GRATEFULLY OUT:

TODAY I AM GRATEFUL FOR:

NOTES:

NEXT DAY GET AHEAD

DAILY LIFE MAGIC

DATE:
Ⓢ Ⓜ Ⓣ Ⓦ Ⓣ Ⓕ Ⓢ

JOY LEVEL

😄 🙂 😐 🙁 😢

QUOTE FOR TODAY

TODAY'S INTENTIONS

REMINDER TO:

INSPIRED THOUGHTS:

TODAY'S PRIORITIES:

EXERCISE:

TOTAL MINUTES:	
TOTAL STEPS:	

WATER INTAKE:

💧 💧 💧 💧 💧 💧 💧

MEAL TRACKER:

BREAKFAST:	LUNCH:
DINNER:	SNACKS:

TO CALL OR EMAIL:

MONEY

MANIFESTED:	GRATEFULLY OUT:

TODAY I AM GRATEFUL FOR:

NOTES:

NEXT DAY GET AHEAD

DAILY LIFE MAGIC

DATE:
(S) (M) (T) (W) (T) (F) (S)

JOY LEVEL

TODAY'S INTENTIONS

REMINDER TO:

QUOTE FOR TODAY

INSPIRED THOUGHTS:

TODAY'S PRIORITES:

EXERCISE:

TOTAL MINUTES:	
TOTAL STEPS:	

WATER INTAKE:

MEAL TRACKER:

BREAKFAST:	LUNCH:
DINNER:	SNACKS:

TO CALL OR EMAIL:

MONEY

MANIFESTED:	GRATEFULLY OUT:

TODAY I AM GRATEFUL FOR:

NOTES:

NEXT DAY GET AHEAD

DAILY LIFE MAGIC

DATE:

Ⓢ Ⓜ Ⓣ Ⓦ Ⓣ Ⓕ Ⓢ

JOY LEVEL

😊 🙂 😐 🙁 😢

QUOTE FOR TODAY

TODAY'S INTENTIONS

REMINDER TO:

INSPIRED THOUGHTS:

TODAY'S PRIORITES:

EXERCISE:

TOTAL MINUTES:	
TOTAL STEPS:	

WATER INTAKE:

💧💧💧💧💧💧

MEAL TRACKER:

BREAKFAST:	LUNCH:
DINNER:	SNACKS:

TO CALL OR EMAIL:

MONEY

MANIFESTED:	GRATEFULLY OUT:

TODAY I AM GRATEFUL FOR:

NOTES:

NEXT DAY GET AHEAD

DAILY LIFE MAGIC

DATE:

S M T W T F S

JOY LEVEL

QUOTE FOR TODAY

TODAY'S INTENTIONS

REMINDER TO:

INSPIRED THOUGHTS:

TODAY'S PRIORITES:

EXERCISE:

TOTAL MINUTES:	
TOTAL STEPS:	

WATER INTAKE:

MEAL TRACKER:

BREAKFAST:	LUNCH:
DINNER:	SNACKS:

TO CALL OR EMAIL:

MONEY

MANIFESTED:	GRATEFULLY OUT:

TODAY I AM GRATEFUL FOR:

NOTES:

NEXT DAY GET AHEAD

DAILY LIFE MAGIC

DATE:
(S) (M) (T) (W) (T) (F) (S)

JOY LEVEL

QUOTE FOR TODAY

TODAY'S INTENTIONS

REMINDER TO:

INSPIRED THOUGHTS:

TODAY'S PRIORITIES:

EXERCISE:

TOTAL MINUTES:	
TOTAL STEPS:	

WATER INTAKE:

MEAL TRACKER:

BREAKFAST:	LUNCH:
DINNER:	SNACKS:

TO CALL OR EMAIL:

MONEY

MANIFESTED:	GRATEFULLY OUT:

TODAY I AM GRATEFUL FOR:

NOTES:

NEXT DAY GET AHEAD

DAILY LIFE MAGIC

DATE:

JOY LEVEL

TODAY'S INTENTIONS

REMINDER TO:

QUOTE FOR TODAY

INSPIRED THOUGHTS :

TODAY'S PRIORITES:

EXERCISE:

TOTAL MINUTES:	
TOTAL STEPS:	

WATER INTAKE:

MEAL TRACKER:

BREAKFAST:	LUNCH:
DINNER:	SNACKS:

TO CALL OR EMAIL:

MONEY

MANIFESTED:	GRATEFULLY OUT:

TODAY I AM GRATEFUL FOR:

NOTES:

NEXT DAY GET AHEAD

DAILY LIFE MAGIC

DATE:

(S) (M) (T) (W) (T) (F) (S)

JOY LEVEL

TODAY'S INTENTIONS

REMINDER TO:

QUOTE FOR TODAY

INSPIRED THOUGHTS:

TODAY'S PRIORITES:

EXERCISE:

TOTAL MINUTES:	
TOTAL STEPS:	

WATER INTAKE:

MEAL TRACKER:

BREAKFAST:	LUNCH:
DINNER:	SNACKS:

TO CALL OR EMAIL:

MONEY

MANIFESTED:	GRATEFULLY OUT:

TODAY I AM GRATEFUL FOR:

NOTES:

NEXT DAY GET AHEAD

DAILY LIFE MAGIC

DATE:

(S) (M) (T) (W) (T) (F) (S)

JOY LEVEL

TODAY'S INTENTIONS

REMINDER TO:

QUOTE FOR TODAY

TODAY'S PRIORITES:

INSPIRED THOUGHTS:

EXERCISE:

TOTAL MINUTES:	
TOTAL STEPS:	

WATER INTAKE:

MEAL TRACKER:

BREAKFAST:	LUNCH:
DINNER:	SNACKS:

TO CALL OR EMAIL:

MONEY

MANIFESTED:	GRATEFULLY OUT:

TODAY I AM GRATEFUL FOR:

NOTES:

NEXT DAY GET AHEAD

DAILY LIFE MAGIC

DATE:
Ⓢ Ⓜ Ⓣ Ⓦ Ⓣ Ⓕ Ⓢ

JOY LEVEL
😊 🙂 😐 🙁 😢

TODAY'S INTENTIONS

REMINDER TO:

QUOTE FOR TODAY

INSPIRED THOUGHTS:

TODAY'S PRIORITES:

EXERCISE:

TOTAL MINUTES:	
TOTAL STEPS:	

WATER INTAKE:
💧 💧 💧 💧 💧 💧

MEAL TRACKER:

BREAKFAST:	LUNCH:
DINNER:	SNACKS:

TO CALL OR EMAIL:

MONEY

MANIFESTED:	GRATEFULLY OUT:

TODAY I AM GRATEFUL FOR:

NOTES:

NEXT DAY GET AHEAD

DAILY LIFE MAGIC

DATE:
Ⓢ Ⓜ Ⓣ Ⓦ Ⓣ Ⓕ Ⓢ

JOY LEVEL

TODAY'S INTENTIONS

REMINDER TO:

QUOTE FOR TODAY

INSPIRED THOUGHTS :

TODAY'S PRIORITES:

EXERCISE:

TOTAL MINUTES:	
TOTAL STEPS:	

WATER INTAKE:

💧💧💧💧💧💧

MEAL TRACKER:

BREAKFAST:	LUNCH:
DINNER:	SNACKS:

TO CALL OR EMAIL:

MONEY

MANIFESTED:	GRATEFULLY OUT:

TODAY I AM GRATEFUL FOR:

NOTES:

NEXT DAY GET AHEAD

DAILY LIFE MAGIC

DATE:
(S) (M) (T) (W) (T) (F) (S)

JOY LEVEL

TODAY'S INTENTIONS

REMINDER TO:

QUOTE FOR TODAY

INSPIRED THOUGHTS:

TODAY'S PRIORITES:

EXERCISE:

TOTAL MINUTES:	
TOTAL STEPS:	

WATER INTAKE:

MEAL TRACKER:

BREAKFAST:	LUNCH:
DINNER:	SNACKS:

TO CALL OR EMAIL:

MONEY

MANIFESTED:	GRATEFULLY OUT:

TODAY I AM GRATEFUL FOR:

NOTES:

NEXT DAY GET AHEAD

DAILY LIFE MAGIC

DATE:

(S) (M) (T) (W) (T) (F) (S)

JOY LEVEL

TODAY'S INTENTIONS

REMINDER TO:

QUOTE FOR TODAY

INSPIRED THOUGHTS:

TODAY'S PRIORITES:

EXERCISE:

TOTAL MINUTES:	
TOTAL STEPS:	

WATER INTAKE:

◊ ◊ ◊ ◊ ◊ ◊ ◊

MEAL TRACKER:

BREAKFAST:	LUNCH:
DINNER:	SNACKS:

TO CALL OR EMAIL:

MONEY

MANIFESTED:	GRATEFULLY OUT:

TODAY I AM GRATEFUL FOR:

NOTES:

NEXT DAY GET AHEAD

DAILY LIFE MAGIC

DATE:

(S) (M) (T) (W) (T) (F) (S)

JOY LEVEL

TODAY'S INTENTIONS

REMINDER TO:

QUOTE FOR TODAY

INSPIRED THOUGHTS:

TODAY'S PRIORITES:

EXERCISE:

TOTAL MINUTES:	
TOTAL STEPS:	

WATER INTAKE:

MEAL TRACKER:

BREAKFAST:	LUNCH:
DINNER:	SNACKS:

TO CALL OR EMAIL:

MONEY

MANIFESTED:	GRATEFULLY OUT:

TODAY I AM GRATEFUL FOR:

NOTES:

NEXT DAY GET AHEAD

DAILY LIFE MAGIC

DATE:

JOY LEVEL

TODAY'S INTENTIONS

REMINDER TO:

QUOTE FOR TODAY

INSPIRED THOUGHTS:

TODAY'S PRIORITES:

EXERCISE:

TOTAL MINUTES:	
TOTAL STEPS:	

WATER INTAKE:

MEAL TRACKER:

BREAKFAST:	LUNCH:
DINNER:	SNACKS:

TO CALL OR EMAIL:

MONEY

MANIFESTED:	GRATEFULLY OUT:

TODAY I AM GRATEFUL FOR:

NOTES:

NEXT DAY GET AHEAD

DAILY LIFE MAGIC

DATE:

Ⓢ Ⓜ Ⓣ Ⓦ Ⓣ Ⓕ Ⓢ

JOY LEVEL

😊 🙂 😐 🙁 😢

TODAY'S INTENTIONS

REMINDER TO:

QUOTE FOR TODAY

INSPIRED THOUGHTS:

TODAY'S PRIORITES:

EXERCISE:

TOTAL MINUTES:	
TOTAL STEPS:	

WATER INTAKE:

💧 💧 💧 💧 💧 💧 💧

MEAL TRACKER:

BREAKFAST:	LUNCH:
DINNER:	SNACKS:

TO CALL OR EMAIL:

MONEY

MANIFESTED:	GRATEFULLY OUT:

TODAY I AM GRATEFUL FOR:

NOTES:

NEXT DAY GET AHEAD

DAILY LIFE MAGIC

DATE:

(S) (M) (T) (W) (T) (F) (S)

JOY LEVEL

TODAY'S INTENTIONS

REMINDER TO:

QUOTE FOR TODAY

INSPIRED THOUGHTS:

TODAY'S PRIORITES:

EXERCISE:

TOTAL MINUTES:	
TOTAL STEPS:	

WATER INTAKE:

MEAL TRACKER:

BREAKFAST:	LUNCH:
DINNER:	SNACKS:

TO CALL OR EMAIL:

MONEY

MANIFESTED:	GRATEFULLY OUT:

TODAY I AM GRATEFUL FOR:

NOTES:

NEXT DAY GET AHEAD

DAILY LIFE MAGIC

DATE:
(S) (M) (T) (W) (T) (F) (S)

JOY LEVEL

QUOTE FOR TODAY

TODAY'S INTENTIONS

REMINDER TO:

INSPIRED THOUGHTS:

TODAY'S PRIORITES:

EXERCISE:

TOTAL MINUTES:	
TOTAL STEPS:	

WATER INTAKE:

MEAL TRACKER:

BREAKFAST:	LUNCH:
DINNER:	SNACKS:

TO CALL OR EMAIL:

MONEY

MANIFESTED:	GRATEFULLY OUT:

TODAY I AM GRATEFUL FOR:

NOTES:

NEXT DAY GET AHEAD

DAILY LIFE MAGIC

DATE:
(S) (M) (T) (W) (T) (F) (S)

JOY LEVEL

TODAY'S INTENTIONS

REMINDER TO:

QUOTE FOR TODAY

INSPIRED THOUGHTS:

TODAY'S PRIORITES:

EXERCISE:

| TOTAL MINUTES: | |
| TOTAL STEPS: | |

WATER INTAKE:

○ ○ ○ ○ ○ ○ ○

MEAL TRACKER:

| BREAKFAST: | LUNCH: |
| DINNER: | SNACKS: |

TO CALL OR EMAIL:

MONEY

| MANIFESTED: | GRATEFULLY OUT: |

TODAY I AM GRATEFUL FOR:

NOTES:

NEXT DAY GET AHEAD

DAILY LIFE MAGIC

DATE:

(S) (M) (T) (W) (T) (F) (S)

JOY LEVEL

TODAY'S INTENTIONS

REMINDER TO:

QUOTE FOR TODAY

TODAY'S PRIORITES:

INSPIRED THOUGHTS:

EXERCISE:

TOTAL MINUTES:	
TOTAL STEPS:	

WATER INTAKE:

MEAL TRACKER:

BREAKFAST:	LUNCH:
DINNER:	SNACKS:

TO CALL OR EMAIL:

MONEY

MANIFESTED:	GRATEFULLY OUT:

TODAY I AM GRATEFUL FOR:

NOTES:

NEXT DAY GET AHEAD

DAILY LIFE MAGIC

DATE:
(S) (M) (T) (W) (T) (F) (S)

JOY LEVEL

TODAY'S INTENTIONS

REMINDER TO:

QUOTE FOR TODAY

INSPIRED THOUGHTS :

TODAY'S PRIORITES:

EXERCISE:

TOTAL MINUTES:	
TOTAL STEPS:	

WATER INTAKE:
◇ ◇ ◇ ◇ ◇ ◇ ◇

MEAL TRACKER:

BREAKFAST:	LUNCH:
DINNER:	SNACKS:

TO CALL OR EMAIL:

MONEY

MANIFESTED:	GRATEFULLY OUT:

TODAY I AM GRATEFUL FOR:

NOTES:

NEXT DAY GET AHEAD

DAILY LIFE MAGIC

DATE:
(S) (M) (T) (W) (T) (F) (S)

JOY LEVEL

TODAY'S INTENTIONS

REMINDER TO:

QUOTE FOR TODAY

TODAY'S PRIORITES:

INSPIRED THOUGHTS :

EXERCISE:

TOTAL MINUTES:	
TOTAL STEPS:	

WATER INTAKE:

MEAL TRACKER:

BREAKFAST:	LUNCH:
DINNER:	SNACKS:

TO CALL OR EMAIL:

MONEY

MANIFESTED:	GRATEFULLY OUT:

TODAY I AM GRATEFUL FOR:

NOTES:

NEXT DAY GET AHEAD

DAILY LIFE MAGIC

DATE:
Ⓢ Ⓜ Ⓣ Ⓦ Ⓣ Ⓕ Ⓢ

JOY LEVEL

TODAY'S INTENTIONS

REMINDER TO:

QUOTE FOR TODAY

INSPIRED THOUGHTS:

TODAY'S PRIORITES:

EXERCISE:

TOTAL MINUTES:	
TOTAL STEPS:	

WATER INTAKE:
💧💧💧💧💧💧💧

MEAL TRACKER:

BREAKFAST:	LUNCH:
DINNER:	SNACKS:

TO CALL OR EMAIL:

MONEY

MANIFESTED:	GRATEFULLY OUT:

TODAY I AM GRATEFUL FOR:

NOTES:

NEXT DAY GET AHEAD

DAILY LIFE MAGIC

DATE:
(S) (M) (T) (W) (T) (F) (S)

JOY LEVEL

TODAY'S INTENTIONS

REMINDER TO:

QUOTE FOR TODAY

TODAY'S PRIORITES:

INSPIRED THOUGHTS :

EXERCISE:

TOTAL MINUTES:	
TOTAL STEPS:	

WATER INTAKE:

MEAL TRACKER:

BREAKFAST:	LUNCH:
DINNER:	SNACKS:

TO CALL OR EMAIL:

MONEY

MANIFESTED:	GRATEFULLY OUT:

TODAY I AM GRATEFUL FOR:

NOTES:

NEXT DAY GET AHEAD

DAILY LIFE MAGIC

DATE:

(S) (M) (T) (W) (T) (F) (S)

JOY LEVEL

TODAY'S INTENTIONS

REMINDER TO:

QUOTE FOR TODAY

INSPIRED THOUGHTS :

TODAY'S PRIORITES:

EXERCISE:

TOTAL MINUTES:	
TOTAL STEPS:	

WATER INTAKE:

○ ○ ○ ○ ○ ○ ○

MEAL TRACKER:

BREAKFAST:	LUNCH:
DINNER:	SNACKS:

TO CALL OR EMAIL:

MONEY

MANIFESTED:	GRATEFULLY OUT:

TODAY I AM GRATEFUL FOR:

NOTES:

NEXT DAY GET AHEAD

DAILY LIFE MAGIC

DATE:

(S) (M) (T) (W) (T) (F) (S)

JOY LEVEL

TODAY'S INTENTIONS

REMINDER TO:

QUOTE FOR TODAY

EXERCISE:

TOTAL MINUTES:	
TOTAL STEPS:	

WATER INTAKE:

TODAY'S PRIORITIES:

INSPIRED THOUGHTS:

MEAL TRACKER:

BREAKFAST:	LUNCH:
DINNER:	SNACKS:

TO CALL OR EMAIL:

MONEY

MANIFESTED:	GRATEFULLY OUT:

TODAY I AM GRATEFUL FOR:

NOTES:

NEXT DAY GET AHEAD

DAILY LIFE MAGIC

DATE:
S M T W T F S

JOY LEVEL

TODAY'S INTENTIONS

REMINDER TO:

QUOTE FOR TODAY

INSPIRED THOUGHTS:

TODAY'S PRIORITES:

EXERCISE:

TOTAL MINUTES:	
TOTAL STEPS:	

WATER INTAKE:

MEAL TRACKER:

TO CALL OR EMAIL:

MONEY

BREAKFAST:	LUNCH:
DINNER:	SNACKS:

MANIFESTED:	GRATEFULLY OUT:

TODAY I AM GRATEFUL FOR:

NOTES:

NEXT DAY GET AHEAD

DAILY LIFE MAGIC

DATE:

Ⓢ Ⓜ Ⓣ Ⓦ Ⓣ Ⓕ Ⓢ

JOY LEVEL

😊 🙂 😐 🙁 😢

QUOTE FOR TODAY

TODAY'S INTENTIONS

REMINDER TO:

INSPIRED THOUGHTS:

TODAY'S PRIORITIES:

EXERCISE:

TOTAL MINUTES:	
TOTAL STEPS:	

WATER INTAKE:

💧💧💧💧💧💧💧

MEAL TRACKER:

BREAKFAST:	LUNCH:
DINNER:	SNACKS:

TO CALL OR EMAIL:

MONEY

MANIFESTED:	GRATEFULLY OUT:

TODAY I AM GRATEFUL FOR:

NOTES:

NEXT DAY GET AHEAD

DAILY LIFE MAGIC

DATE:

(S) (M) (T) (W) (T) (F) (S)

JOY LEVEL

TODAY'S INTENTIONS

REMINDER TO:

QUOTE FOR TODAY

INSPIRED THOUGHTS :

TODAY'S PRIORITES:

EXERCISE:

TOTAL MINUTES:	
TOTAL STEPS:	

WATER INTAKE:

MEAL TRACKER:

BREAKFAST:	LUNCH:
DINNER:	SNACKS:

TO CALL OR EMAIL:

MONEY

MANIFESTED:	GRATEFULLY OUT:

TODAY I AM GRATEFUL FOR:

NOTES:

NEXT DAY GET AHEAD

DAILY LIFE MAGIC

DATE:

JOY LEVEL

TODAY'S INTENTIONS

REMINDER TO:

QUOTE FOR TODAY

INSPIRED THOUGHTS :

TODAY'S PRIORITIES:

EXERCISE:

TOTAL MINUTES:	
TOTAL STEPS:	

WATER INTAKE:

◯ ◯ ◯ ◯ ◯ ◯ ◯

MEAL TRACKER:

TO CALL OR EMAIL:

MONEY

BREAKFAST:	LUNCH:
DINNER:	SNACKS:

MANIFESTED:	GRATEFULLY OUT:

TODAY I AM GRATEFUL FOR:

NOTES:

NEXT DAY GET AHEAD

DAILY LIFE MAGIC

DATE:
Ⓢ Ⓜ Ⓣ Ⓦ Ⓣ Ⓕ Ⓢ

JOY LEVEL

TODAY'S INTENTIONS

REMINDER TO:

QUOTE FOR TODAY

INSPIRED THOUGHTS :

TODAY'S PRIORITIES:

EXERCISE:

TOTAL MINUTES:	
TOTAL STEPS:	

WATER INTAKE:
○ ○ ○ ○ ○ ○ ○

MEAL TRACKER:

BREAKFAST:	LUNCH:
DINNER:	SNACKS:

TO CALL OR EMAIL:

MONEY

MANIFESTED:	GRATEFULLY OUT:

TODAY I AM GRATEFUL FOR:

NOTES:

NEXT DAY GET AHEAD

DAILY LIFE MAGIC

DATE:

Ⓢ Ⓜ Ⓣ Ⓦ Ⓣ Ⓕ Ⓢ

JOY LEVEL

😄 🙂 😐 🙁 😢

QUOTE FOR TODAY

TODAY'S INTENTIONS

REMINDER TO:

INSPIRED THOUGHTS:

EXERCISE:

TOTAL MINUTES:	
TOTAL STEPS:	

TODAY'S PRIORITES:

WATER INTAKE:

💧 💧 💧 💧 💧 💧

MEAL TRACKER:

BREAKFAST:	LUNCH:
DINNER:	SNACKS:

TO CALL OR EMAIL:

MONEY

MANIFESTED:	GRATEFULLY OUT:

TODAY I AM GRATEFUL FOR:

NOTES:

NEXT DAY GET AHEAD

DAILY LIFE MAGIC

DATE:

S   T F

JOY LEVEL

TODAY'S INTENTIONS

REMINDER TO:

QUOTE FOR TODAY

INSPIRED THOUGHTS :

TODAY'S PRIORITES:

EXERCISE:

TOTAL MINUTES:	
TOTAL STEPS:	

WATER INTAKE:

◯ ◯ ◯ ◯ ◯ ◯ ◯

MEAL TRACKER:

BREAKFAST:	LUNCH:
DINNER:	SNACKS:

TO CALL OR EMAIL:

MONEY

MANIFESTED:	GRATEFULLY OUT:

TODAY I AM GRATEFUL FOR:

NOTES:

NEXT DAY GET AHEAD

DAILY LIFE MAGIC

DATE:
Ⓢ Ⓜ Ⓣ Ⓦ Ⓣ Ⓕ Ⓢ

JOY LEVEL

😊 🙂 😐 🙁 😢

QUOTE FOR TODAY

TODAY'S INTENTIONS

REMINDER TO:

INSPIRED THOUGHTS:

TODAY'S PRIORITES:

EXERCISE:

TOTAL MINUTES:	
TOTAL STEPS:	

WATER INTAKE:

💧💧💧💧💧💧

MEAL TRACKER:

BREAKFAST:	LUNCH:
DINNER:	SNACKS:

TO CALL OR EMAIL:

MONEY

MANIFESTED:	GRATEFULLY OUT:

TODAY I AM GRATEFUL FOR:

NOTES:

NEXT DAY GET AHEAD

DAILY LIFE MAGIC

DATE:
Ⓢ Ⓜ Ⓣ Ⓦ Ⓣ Ⓕ Ⓢ

JOY LEVEL

QUOTE FOR TODAY

TODAY'S INTENTIONS

REMINDER TO:

INSPIRED THOUGHTS:

TODAY'S PRIORITES:

EXERCISE:

TOTAL MINUTES:	
TOTAL STEPS:	

WATER INTAKE:
💧💧💧💧💧💧💧

MEAL TRACKER:

BREAKFAST:	LUNCH:
DINNER:	SNACKS:

TO CALL OR EMAIL:

MONEY

MANIFESTED:	GRATEFULLY OUT:

TODAY I AM GRATEFUL FOR:

NOTES:

NEXT DAY GET AHEAD

DAILY LIFE MAGIC

DATE:
S M T W T F S

JOY LEVEL

TODAY'S INTENTIONS

REMINDER TO:

QUOTE FOR TODAY

INSPIRED THOUGHTS:

TODAY'S PRIORITES:

EXERCISE:

TOTAL MINUTES:	
TOTAL STEPS:	

WATER INTAKE:

MEAL TRACKER:

BREAKFAST:	LUNCH:
DINNER:	SNACKS:

TO CALL OR EMAIL:

MONEY

MANIFESTED:	GRATEFULLY OUT:

TODAY I AM GRATEFUL FOR:

NOTES:

NEXT DAY GET AHEAD

DAILY LIFE MAGIC

DATE:

(S) (M) (T) (W) (T) (F) (S)

JOY LEVEL

TODAY'S INTENTIONS

REMINDER TO:

QUOTE FOR TODAY

TODAY'S PRIORITES:

INSPIRED THOUGHTS:

EXERCISE:

TOTAL MINUTES:	
TOTAL STEPS:	

WATER INTAKE:

◊ ◊ ◊ ◊ ◊ ◊ ◊

MEAL TRACKER:

BREAKFAST:	LUNCH:
DINNER:	SNACKS:

TO CALL OR EMAIL:

MONEY

MANIFESTED:	GRATEFULLY OUT:

TODAY I AM GRATEFUL FOR:

NOTES:

NEXT DAY GET AHEAD

DAILY LIFE MAGIC

DATE:

(S) (M) (T) (W) (T) (F) (S)

JOY LEVEL

😊 🙂 😐 🙁 😢

QUOTE FOR TODAY

TODAY'S INTENTIONS

REMINDER TO:

INSPIRED THOUGHTS:

TODAY'S PRIORITES:

EXERCISE:

TOTAL MINUTES:	
TOTAL STEPS:	

WATER INTAKE:

💧💧💧💧💧💧💧

MEAL TRACKER:

BREAKFAST:	LUNCH:
DINNER:	SNACKS:

TO CALL OR EMAIL:

MONEY

MANIFESTED:	GRATEFULLY OUT:

TODAY I AM GRATEFUL FOR:

NOTES:

NEXT DAY GET AHEAD

DAILY LIFE MAGIC

DATE:

JOY LEVEL

TODAY'S INTENTIONS

REMINDER TO:

QUOTE FOR TODAY

TODAY'S PRIORITES:

INSPIRED THOUGHTS :

EXERCISE:

TOTAL MINUTES:	
TOTAL STEPS:	

WATER INTAKE:

MEAL TRACKER:

BREAKFAST:	LUNCH:
DINNER:	SNACKS:

TO CALL OR EMAIL:

MONEY

MANIFESTED:	GRATEFULLY OUT:

TODAY I AM GRATEFUL FOR:

NOTES:

NEXT DAY GET AHEAD

DAILY LIFE MAGIC

DATE:

(S) (M) (T) (W) (T) (F) (S)

JOY LEVEL

TODAY'S INTENTIONS

REMINDER TO:

QUOTE FOR TODAY

INSPIRED THOUGHTS:

TODAY'S PRIORITES:

EXERCISE:

TOTAL MINUTES:	
TOTAL STEPS:	

WATER INTAKE:

MEAL TRACKER:

BREAKFAST:	LUNCH:
DINNER:	SNACKS:

TO CALL OR EMAIL:

MONEY

MANIFESTED:	GRATEFULLY OUT:

TODAY I AM GRATEFUL FOR:

NOTES:

NEXT DAY GET AHEAD

DAILY LIFE MAGIC

DATE:

Ⓢ Ⓜ Ⓣ Ⓦ Ⓣ Ⓕ Ⓢ

JOY LEVEL

TODAY'S INTENTIONS

REMINDER TO:

QUOTE FOR TODAY

INSPIRED THOUGHTS:

TODAY'S PRIORITES:

EXERCISE:

TOTAL MINUTES:	
TOTAL STEPS:	

WATER INTAKE:

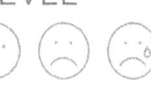

MEAL TRACKER:

BREAKFAST:	LUNCH:
DINNER:	SNACKS:

TO CALL OR EMAIL:

MONEY

MANIFESTED:	GRATEFULLY OUT:

TODAY I AM GRATEFUL FOR:

NOTES:

NEXT DAY GET AHEAD

DAILY LIFE MAGIC

DATE:
(S) (M) (T) (W) (T) (F) (S)

JOY LEVEL

TODAY'S INTENTIONS

REMINDER TO:

QUOTE FOR TODAY

TODAY'S PRIORITES:

INSPIRED THOUGHTS:

EXERCISE:

TOTAL MINUTES:	
TOTAL STEPS:	

WATER INTAKE:

MEAL TRACKER:

BREAKFAST:	LUNCH:
DINNER:	SNACKS:

TO CALL OR EMAIL:

MONEY

MANIFESTED:	GRATEFULLY OUT:

TODAY I AM GRATEFUL FOR:

NOTES:

NEXT DAY GET AHEAD

DAILY LIFE MAGIC

DATE:

(S) (M) (T) (W) (T) (F) (S)

JOY LEVEL

TODAY'S INTENTIONS

REMINDER TO:

QUOTE FOR TODAY

TODAY'S PRIORITES:

INSPIRED THOUGHTS :

EXERCISE:

TOTAL MINUTES:	
TOTAL STEPS:	

WATER INTAKE:

○ ○ ○ ○ ○ ○ ○

MEAL TRACKER:

BREAKFAST:	LUNCH:
DINNER:	SNACKS:

TO CALL OR EMAIL:

MONEY

MANIFESTED:	GRATEFULLY OUT:

TODAY I AM GRATEFUL FOR:

NOTES:

NEXT DAY GET AHEAD

DAILY LIFE MAGIC

DATE:

Ⓢ Ⓜ Ⓣ Ⓦ Ⓣ Ⓕ Ⓢ

JOY LEVEL

TODAY'S INTENTIONS

REMINDER TO:

QUOTE FOR TODAY

TODAY'S PRIORITES:

INSPIRED THOUGHTS:

EXERCISE:

TOTAL MINUTES:	
TOTAL STEPS:	

WATER INTAKE:

💧 💧 💧 💧 💧 💧 💧

MEAL TRACKER:

BREAKFAST:	LUNCH:
DINNER:	SNACKS:

TO CALL OR EMAIL:

MONEY

MANIFESTED:	GRATEFULLY OUT:

TODAY I AM GRATEFUL FOR:

NOTES:

NEXT DAY GET AHEAD

DAILY LIFE MAGIC

DATE:

JOY LEVEL

TODAY'S INTENTIONS

REMINDER TO:

QUOTE FOR TODAY

INSPIRED THOUGHTS :

TODAY'S PRIORITES:

EXERCISE:

TOTAL MINUTES:	
TOTAL STEPS:	

WATER INTAKE:

MEAL TRACKER:

BREAKFAST:	LUNCH:
DINNER:	SNACKS:

TO CALL OR EMAIL:

MONEY

MANIFESTED:	GRATEFULLY OUT:

TODAY I AM GRATEFUL FOR:

NOTES:

NEXT DAY GET AHEAD

DAILY LIFE MAGIC

DATE:
(S) (M) (T) (W) (T) (F) (S)

JOY LEVEL

TODAY'S INTENTIONS

REMINDER TO:

QUOTE FOR TODAY

INSPIRED THOUGHTS:

TODAY'S PRIORITIES:

EXERCISE:

TOTAL MINUTES:	
TOTAL STEPS:	

WATER INTAKE:

MEAL TRACKER:

BREAKFAST:	LUNCH:
DINNER:	SNACKS:

TO CALL OR EMAIL:

MONEY

MANIFESTED:	GRATEFULLY OUT:

TODAY I AM GRATEFUL FOR:

NOTES:

NEXT DAY GET AHEAD

DAILY LIFE MAGIC

DATE:

Ⓢ Ⓜ Ⓣ Ⓦ Ⓣ Ⓕ Ⓢ

JOY LEVEL

TODAY'S INTENTIONS

REMINDER TO:

QUOTE FOR TODAY

TODAY'S PRIORITIES:

INSPIRED THOUGHTS:

EXERCISE:

TOTAL MINUTES:	
TOTAL STEPS:	

WATER INTAKE:

◯ ◯ ◯ ◯ ◯ ◯ ◯

MEAL TRACKER:

BREAKFAST:	LUNCH:
DINNER:	SNACKS:

TO CALL OR EMAIL:

MONEY

MANIFESTED:	GRATEFULLY OUT:

TODAY I AM GRATEFUL FOR:

NOTES:

NEXT DAY GET AHEAD

DAILY LIFE MAGIC

DATE:

Ⓢ Ⓜ Ⓣ Ⓦ Ⓣ Ⓕ Ⓢ

JOY LEVEL

😁 🙂 😐 🙁 😢

QUOTE FOR TODAY

TODAY'S INTENTIONS

REMINDER TO:

INSPIRED THOUGHTS :

TODAY'S PRIORITES:

EXERCISE:

TOTAL MINUTES:	
TOTAL STEPS:	

WATER INTAKE:

💧💧💧💧💧💧💧

MEAL TRACKER:

BREAKFAST:	LUNCH:
DINNER:	SNACKS:

TO CALL OR EMAIL:

MONEY

MANIFESTED:	GRATEFULLY OUT:

TODAY I AM GRATEFUL FOR:

NOTES:

NEXT DAY GET AHEAD

DAILY LIFE MAGIC

DATE:

JOY LEVEL

TODAY'S INTENTIONS

REMINDER TO:

QUOTE FOR TODAY

INSPIRED THOUGHTS:

TODAY'S PRIORITES:

EXERCISE:

TOTAL MINUTES:	
TOTAL STEPS:	

WATER INTAKE:

MEAL TRACKER:

TO CALL OR EMAIL:

MONEY

BREAKFAST:	LUNCH:
DINNER:	SNACKS:

MANIFESTED:	GRATEFULLY OUT:

TODAY I AM GRATEFUL FOR:

NOTES:

NEXT DAY GET AHEAD

DAILY LIFE MAGIC

DATE:

(S) (M) (T) (W) (T) (F) (S)

JOY LEVEL

TODAY'S INTENTIONS

REMINDER TO:

QUOTE FOR TODAY

TODAY'S PRIORITES:

INSPIRED THOUGHTS:

EXERCISE:

TOTAL MINUTES:	
TOTAL STEPS:	

WATER INTAKE:

◊ ◊ ◊ ◊ ◊ ◊ ◊

MEAL TRACKER:

BREAKFAST:	LUNCH:
DINNER:	SNACKS:

TO CALL OR EMAIL:

MONEY

MANIFESTED:	GRATEFULLY OUT:

TODAY I AM GRATEFUL FOR:

NOTES:

NEXT DAY GET AHEAD

DAILY LIFE MAGIC

DATE:

JOY LEVEL

TODAY'S INTENTIONS

REMINDER TO:

QUOTE FOR TODAY

INSPIRED THOUGHTS:

TODAY'S PRIORITES:

EXERCISE:

TOTAL MINUTES:	
TOTAL STEPS:	

WATER INTAKE:

MEAL TRACKER:

BREAKFAST:	LUNCH:
DINNER:	SNACKS:

TO CALL OR EMAIL:

MONEY

MANIFESTED:	GRATEFULLY OUT:

TODAY I AM GRATEFUL FOR:

NOTES:

NEXT DAY GET AHEAD

DAILY LIFE MAGIC

DATE:
Ⓢ Ⓜ Ⓣ Ⓦ Ⓣ Ⓕ Ⓢ

JOY LEVEL

TODAY'S INTENTIONS

REMINDER TO:

QUOTE FOR TODAY

INSPIRED THOUGHTS:

TODAY'S PRIORITES:

EXERCISE:

TOTAL MINUTES:	
TOTAL STEPS:	

WATER INTAKE:

◊ ◊ ◊ ◊ ◊ ◊

MEAL TRACKER:

BREAKFAST:	LUNCH:
DINNER:	SNACKS:

TO CALL OR EMAIL:

MONEY

MANIFESTED:	GRATEFULLY OUT:

TODAY I AM GRATEFUL FOR:

NOTES:

NEXT DAY GET AHEAD

DAILY LIFE MAGIC

DATE:

(S) (M) (T) (W) (T) (F) (S)

JOY LEVEL

TODAY'S INTENTIONS

REMINDER TO:

QUOTE FOR TODAY

TODAY'S PRIORITES:

INSPIRED THOUGHTS :

EXERCISE:

TOTAL MINUTES:	
TOTAL STEPS:	

WATER INTAKE:

MEAL TRACKER:

BREAKFAST:	LUNCH:
DINNER:	SNACKS:

TO CALL OR EMAIL:

MONEY

MANIFESTED:	GRATEFULLY OUT:

TODAY I AM GRATEFUL FOR:

NOTES:

NEXT DAY GET AHEAD

DAILY LIFE MAGIC

DATE:
(S) (M) (T) (W) (T) (F) (S)

JOY LEVEL

TODAY'S INTENTIONS

REMINDER TO:

QUOTE FOR TODAY

INSPIRED THOUGHTS:

TODAY'S PRIORITIES:

EXERCISE:

TOTAL MINUTES:	
TOTAL STEPS:	

WATER INTAKE:

MEAL TRACKER:

BREAKFAST:	LUNCH:
DINNER:	SNACKS:

TO CALL OR EMAIL:

MONEY

MANIFESTED:	GRATEFULLY OUT:

TODAY I AM GRATEFUL FOR:

NOTES:

NEXT DAY GET AHEAD

DAILY LIFE MAGIC

DATE:

(S)(M)(T)(W)(T)(F)(S)

JOY LEVEL

TODAY'S INTENTIONS

REMINDER TO:

QUOTE FOR TODAY

INSPIRED THOUGHTS :

TODAY'S PRIORITES:

EXERCISE:

TOTAL MINUTES:	
TOTAL STEPS:	

WATER INTAKE:

MEAL TRACKER:

BREAKFAST:	LUNCH:
DINNER:	SNACKS:

TO CALL OR EMAIL:

MONEY

MANIFESTED:	GRATEFULLY OUT:

TODAY I AM GRATEFUL FOR:

NOTES:

NEXT DAY GET AHEAD

DAILY LIFE MAGIC

DATE:
(S) (M) (T) (W) (T) (F) (S)

JOY LEVEL

TODAY'S INTENTIONS

REMINDER TO:

QUOTE FOR TODAY

INSPIRED THOUGHTS:

TODAY'S PRIORITES:

EXERCISE:

TOTAL MINUTES:	
TOTAL STEPS:	

WATER INTAKE:

MEAL TRACKER:

BREAKFAST:	LUNCH:
DINNER:	SNACKS:

TO CALL OR EMAIL:

MONEY

MANIFESTED:	GRATEFULLY OUT:

TODAY I AM GRATEFUL FOR:

NOTES:

NEXT DAY GET AHEAD

DAILY LIFE MAGIC

DATE:

JOY LEVEL

TODAY'S INTENTIONS

REMINDER TO:

QUOTE FOR TODAY

INSPIRED THOUGHTS :

TODAY'S PRIORITES:

EXERCISE:

TOTAL MINUTES:	
TOTAL STEPS:	

WATER INTAKE:

◯ ◯ ◯ ◯ ◯ ◯ ◯

MEAL TRACKER:

BREAKFAST:	LUNCH:
DINNER:	SNACKS:

TO CALL OR EMAIL:

MONEY

MANIFESTED:	GRATEFULLY OUT:

TODAY I AM GRATEFUL FOR:

NOTES:

NEXT DAY GET AHEAD

DAILY LIFE MAGIC

DATE:
(S) (M) (T) (W) (T) (F) (S)

JOY LEVEL

TODAY'S INTENTIONS

REMINDER TO:

QUOTE FOR TODAY

INSPIRED THOUGHTS:

TODAY'S PRIORITES:

EXERCISE:

TOTAL MINUTES:	
TOTAL STEPS:	

WATER INTAKE:

MEAL TRACKER:

BREAKFAST:	LUNCH:
DINNER:	SNACKS:

TO CALL OR EMAIL:

MONEY

MANIFESTED:	GRATEFULLY OUT:

TODAY I AM GRATEFUL FOR:

NOTES:

NEXT DAY GET AHEAD

DAILY LIFE MAGIC

DATE:
Ⓢ Ⓜ Ⓣ Ⓦ Ⓣ Ⓕ Ⓢ

JOY LEVEL

TODAY'S INTENTIONS

REMINDER TO:

QUOTE FOR TODAY

INSPIRED THOUGHTS:

TODAY'S PRIORITIES:

EXERCISE:

TOTAL MINUTES:	
TOTAL STEPS:	

WATER INTAKE:
💧💧💧💧💧💧💧

MEAL TRACKER:

BREAKFAST:	LUNCH:
DINNER:	SNACKS:

TO CALL OR EMAIL:

MONEY

MANIFESTED:	GRATEFULLY OUT:

TODAY I AM GRATEFUL FOR:

NOTES:

NEXT DAY GET AHEAD

DAILY LIFE MAGIC

DATE:
(S) (M) (T) (W) (T) (F) (S)

JOY LEVEL

TODAY'S INTENTIONS

REMINDER TO:

QUOTE FOR TODAY

INSPIRED THOUGHTS:

TODAY'S PRIORITIES:

EXERCISE:

TOTAL MINUTES:	
TOTAL STEPS:	

WATER INTAKE:

MEAL TRACKER:

BREAKFAST:	LUNCH:
DINNER:	SNACKS:

TO CALL OR EMAIL:

MONEY

MANIFESTED:	GRATEFULLY OUT:

TODAY I AM GRATEFUL FOR:

NOTES:

NEXT DAY GET AHEAD

DAILY LIFE MAGIC

DATE:
(S) (M) (T) (W) (T) (F) (S)

JOY LEVEL

TODAY'S INTENTIONS

REMINDER TO:

QUOTE FOR TODAY

TODAY'S PRIORITES:

INSPIRED THOUGHTS:

EXERCISE:

TOTAL MINUTES:	
TOTAL STEPS:	

WATER INTAKE:

MEAL TRACKER:

BREAKFAST:	LUNCH:
DINNER:	SNACKS:

TO CALL OR EMAIL:

MONEY

MANIFESTED:	GRATEFULLY OUT:

TODAY I AM GRATEFUL FOR:

NOTES:

NEXT DAY GET AHEAD

DAILY LIFE MAGIC

DATE:

(S) (M) (T) (W) (T) (F) (S)

JOY LEVEL

QUOTE FOR TODAY

TODAY'S INTENTIONS

REMINDER TO:

EXERCISE:

TOTAL MINUTES:	
TOTAL STEPS:	

WATER INTAKE:

○ ○ ○ ○ ○ ○ ○

MEAL TRACKER:

BREAKFAST:	LUNCH:
DINNER:	SNACKS:

TODAY'S PRIORITES:

TO CALL OR EMAIL:

INSPIRED THOUGHTS:

MONEY

MANIFESTED:	GRATEFULLY OUT:

TODAY I AM GRATEFUL FOR:

NOTES:

NEXT DAY GET AHEAD

DAILY LIFE MAGIC

DATE:

Ⓢ Ⓜ Ⓣ Ⓦ Ⓣ Ⓕ Ⓢ

JOY LEVEL

TODAY'S INTENTIONS

REMINDER TO:

QUOTE FOR TODAY

INSPIRED THOUGHTS:

TODAY'S PRIORITES:

EXERCISE:

TOTAL MINUTES:	
TOTAL STEPS:	

WATER INTAKE:

◊ ◊ ◊ ◊ ◊ ◊ ◊

MEAL TRACKER:

TO CALL OR EMAIL:

MONEY

BREAKFAST:	LUNCH:
DINNER:	SNACKS:

MANIFESTED:	GRATEFULLY OUT:

TODAY I AM GRATEFUL FOR:

NOTES:

NEXT DAY GET AHEAD

DAILY LIFE MAGIC

DATE:

Ⓢ Ⓜ Ⓣ Ⓦ Ⓣ Ⓕ Ⓢ

JOY LEVEL

😊 🙂 😐 🙁 😢

TODAY'S INTENTIONS

REMINDER TO:

QUOTE FOR TODAY

TODAY'S PRIORITES:

INSPIRED THOUGHTS:

EXERCISE:

TOTAL MINUTES:	
TOTAL STEPS:	

WATER INTAKE:

💧💧💧💧💧💧

MEAL TRACKER:

BREAKFAST:	LUNCH:
DINNER:	SNACKS:

TO CALL OR EMAIL:

MONEY

MANIFESTED:	GRATEFULLY OUT:

TODAY I AM GRATEFUL FOR:

NOTES:

NEXT DAY GET AHEAD

DAILY LIFE MAGIC

DATE:
Ⓢ Ⓜ Ⓣ Ⓦ Ⓣ Ⓕ Ⓢ

JOY LEVEL

TODAY'S INTENTIONS

REMINDER TO:

QUOTE FOR TODAY

INSPIRED THOUGHTS:

TODAY'S PRIORITES:

EXERCISE:

TOTAL MINUTES:	
TOTAL STEPS:	

WATER INTAKE:
💧💧💧💧💧💧💧

MEAL TRACKER:

BREAKFAST:	LUNCH:
DINNER:	SNACKS:

TO CALL OR EMAIL:

MONEY

MANIFESTED:	GRATEFULLY OUT:

TODAY I AM GRATEFUL FOR:

NOTES:

NEXT DAY GET AHEAD

DAILY LIFE MAGIC

DATE:

(S) (M) (T) (W) (T) (F) (S)

JOY LEVEL

TODAY'S INTENTIONS

REMINDER TO:

QUOTE FOR TODAY

INSPIRED THOUGHTS:

TODAY'S PRIORITIES:

EXERCISE:

TOTAL MINUTES:	
TOTAL STEPS:	

WATER INTAKE:

◊ ◊ ◊ ◊ ◊ ◊ ◊

MEAL TRACKER:

BREAKFAST:	LUNCH:
DINNER:	SNACKS:

TO CALL OR EMAIL:

MONEY

MANIFESTED:	GRATEFULLY OUT:

TODAY I AM GRATEFUL FOR:

NOTES:

NEXT DAY GET AHEAD

DAILY LIFE MAGIC

DATE:
(S) (M) (T) (W) (T) (F) (S)

JOY LEVEL

TODAY'S INTENTIONS

REMINDER TO:

QUOTE FOR TODAY

TODAY'S PRIORITES:

INSPIRED THOUGHTS:

EXERCISE:

TOTAL MINUTES:	
TOTAL STEPS:	

WATER INTAKE:

MEAL TRACKER:

BREAKFAST:	LUNCH:
DINNER:	SNACKS:

TO CALL OR EMAIL:

MONEY

MANIFESTED:	GRATEFULLY OUT:

TODAY I AM GRATEFUL FOR:

NOTES:

NEXT DAY GET AHEAD

DAILY LIFE MAGIC

DATE:

(S) (M) (T) (W) (T) (F) (S)

JOY LEVEL

TODAY'S INTENTIONS

REMINDER TO:

QUOTE FOR TODAY

INSPIRED THOUGHTS:

TODAY'S PRIORITES:

EXERCISE:

TOTAL MINUTES:	
TOTAL STEPS:	

WATER INTAKE:

MEAL TRACKER:

BREAKFAST:	LUNCH:
DINNER:	SNACKS:

TO CALL OR EMAIL:

MONEY

MANIFESTED:	GRATEFULLY OUT:

TODAY I AM GRATEFUL FOR:

NOTES:

NEXT DAY GET AHEAD

DAILY LIFE MAGIC

DATE:
(S) (M) (T) (W) (T) (F) (S)

JOY LEVEL

TODAY'S INTENTIONS

REMINDER TO:

QUOTE FOR TODAY

TODAY'S PRIORITES:

INSPIRED THOUGHTS :

EXERCISE:

TOTAL MINUTES:	
TOTAL STEPS:	

WATER INTAKE:

○ ○ ○ ○ ○ ○ ○

MEAL TRACKER:

BREAKFAST:	LUNCH:
DINNER:	SNACKS:

TO CALL OR EMAIL:

MONEY

MANIFESTED:	GRATEFULLY OUT:

TODAY I AM GRATEFUL FOR:

NOTES:

NEXT DAY GET AHEAD

DAILY LIFE MAGIC

DATE:
Ⓢ Ⓜ Ⓣ Ⓦ Ⓣ Ⓕ Ⓢ

JOY LEVEL

TODAY'S INTENTIONS

REMINDER TO:

QUOTE FOR TODAY

TODAY'S PRIORITES:

INSPIRED THOUGHTS :

EXERCISE:

TOTAL MINUTES:	
TOTAL STEPS:	

WATER INTAKE:

💧 💧 💧 💧 💧 💧 💧

MEAL TRACKER:

BREAKFAST:	LUNCH:
DINNER:	SNACKS:

TO CALL OR EMAIL:

MONEY

MANIFESTED:	GRATEFULLY OUT:

TODAY I AM GRATEFUL FOR:

NOTES:

NEXT DAY GET AHEAD

DAILY LIFE MAGIC

DATE:
Ⓢ Ⓜ Ⓣ Ⓦ Ⓣ Ⓕ Ⓢ

JOY LEVEL

TODAY'S INTENTIONS

REMINDER TO:

QUOTE FOR TODAY

INSPIRED THOUGHTS :

TODAY'S PRIORITIES:

EXERCISE:

TOTAL MINUTES:	
TOTAL STEPS:	

WATER INTAKE:

MEAL TRACKER:

BREAKFAST:	LUNCH:
DINNER:	SNACKS:

TO CALL OR EMAIL:

MONEY

MANIFESTED:	GRATEFULLY OUT:

TODAY I AM GRATEFUL FOR:

NOTES:

NEXT DAY GET AHEAD

DAILY LIFE MAGIC

DATE:
(S) (M) (T) (W) (T) (F) (S)

JOY LEVEL

TODAY'S INTENTIONS

REMINDER TO:

QUOTE FOR TODAY

INSPIRED THOUGHTS:

TODAY'S PRIORITES:

EXERCISE:

TOTAL MINUTES:	
TOTAL STEPS:	

WATER INTAKE:

MEAL TRACKER:

BREAKFAST:	LUNCH:
DINNER:	SNACKS:

TO CALL OR EMAIL:

MONEY

MANIFESTED:	GRATEFULLY OUT:

TODAY I AM GRATEFUL FOR:

NOTES:

NEXT DAY GET AHEAD

DAILY LIFE MAGIC

DATE:

(S) (M) (T) (W) (T) (F) (S)

JOY LEVEL

TODAY'S INTENTIONS

REMINDER TO:

QUOTE FOR TODAY

INSPIRED THOUGHTS:

TODAY'S PRIORITES:

EXERCISE:

TOTAL MINUTES:	
TOTAL STEPS:	

WATER INTAKE:

MEAL TRACKER:

BREAKFAST:	LUNCH:
DINNER:	SNACKS:

TO CALL OR EMAIL:

MONEY

MANIFESTED:	GRATEFULLY OUT:

TODAY I AM GRATEFUL FOR:

NOTES:

NEXT DAY GET AHEAD

DAILY LIFE MAGIC

DATE:
Ⓢ Ⓜ Ⓣ Ⓦ Ⓣ Ⓕ Ⓢ

JOY LEVEL
😁 🙂 😐 🙁 😢

TODAY'S INTENTIONS

REMINDER TO:

QUOTE FOR TODAY

EXERCISE:

TOTAL MINUTES:	
TOTAL STEPS:	

WATER INTAKE:
💧 💧 💧 💧 💧 💧 💧

MEAL TRACKER:

BREAKFAST:	LUNCH:
DINNER:	SNACKS:

TODAY'S PRIORITES:

TO CALL OR EMAIL:

NOTES:

INSPIRED THOUGHTS:

MONEY

MANIFESTED:	GRATEFULLY OUT:

NEXT DAY GET AHEAD

TODAY I AM GRATEFUL FOR:

DAILY LIFE MAGIC

DATE:

JOY LEVEL

TODAY'S INTENTIONS

REMINDER TO:

QUOTE FOR TODAY

INSPIRED THOUGHTS:

TODAY'S PRIORITES:

EXERCISE:

TOTAL MINUTES:	
TOTAL STEPS:	

WATER INTAKE:

MEAL TRACKER:

TO CALL OR EMAIL:

MONEY

BREAKFAST:	LUNCH:
DINNER:	SNACKS:

MANIFESTED:	GRATEFULLY OUT:

TODAY I AM GRATEFUL FOR:

NOTES:

NEXT DAY GET AHEAD

DAILY LIFE MAGIC

DATE:

(S) (M) (T) (W) (T) (F) (S)

JOY LEVEL

TODAY'S INTENTIONS

REMINDER TO:

QUOTE FOR TODAY

TODAY'S PRIORITES:

INSPIRED THOUGHTS:

EXERCISE:

TOTAL MINUTES:	
TOTAL STEPS:	

WATER INTAKE:

MEAL TRACKER:

BREAKFAST:	LUNCH:
DINNER:	SNACKS:

TO CALL OR EMAIL:

MONEY

MANIFESTED:	GRATEFULLY OUT:

TODAY I AM GRATEFUL FOR:

NOTES:

NEXT DAY GET AHEAD

DAILY LIFE MAGIC

DATE:
Ⓢ Ⓜ Ⓣ Ⓦ Ⓣ Ⓕ Ⓢ

JOY LEVEL

TODAY'S INTENTIONS

REMINDER TO:

QUOTE FOR TODAY

TODAY'S PRIORITIES:

INSPIRED THOUGHTS :

EXERCISE:

TOTAL MINUTES:	
TOTAL STEPS:	

WATER INTAKE:
💧💧💧💧💧💧

MEAL TRACKER:

BREAKFAST:	LUNCH:
DINNER:	SNACKS:

TO CALL OR EMAIL:

MONEY

MANIFESTED:	GRATEFULLY OUT:

TODAY I AM GRATEFUL FOR:

NOTES:

NEXT DAY GET AHEAD

DAILY LIFE MAGIC

DATE:
(S) (M) (T) (W) (T) (F) (S)

JOY LEVEL

TODAY'S INTENTIONS

REMINDER TO:

QUOTE FOR TODAY

TODAY'S PRIORITIES:

INSPIRED THOUGHTS:

EXERCISE:

TOTAL MINUTES:	
TOTAL STEPS:	

WATER INTAKE:

MEAL TRACKER:

BREAKFAST:	LUNCH:
DINNER:	SNACKS:

TO CALL OR EMAIL:

MONEY

MANIFESTED:	GRATEFULLY OUT:

TODAY I AM GRATEFUL FOR:

NOTES:

NEXT DAY GET AHEAD

DAILY LIFE MAGIC

DATE:

JOY LEVEL

TODAY'S INTENTIONS

REMINDER TO:

QUOTE FOR TODAY

INSPIRED THOUGHTS:

TODAY'S PRIORITES:

EXERCISE:

TOTAL MINUTES:	
TOTAL STEPS:	

WATER INTAKE:

MEAL TRACKER:

BREAKFAST:	LUNCH:
DINNER:	SNACKS:

TO CALL OR EMAIL:

MONEY

MANIFESTED:	GRATEFULLY OUT:

TODAY I AM GRATEFUL FOR:

NOTES:

NEXT DAY GET AHEAD

DAILY LIFE MAGIC

DATE:

(S) (M) (T) (W) (T) (F) (S)

JOY LEVEL

TODAY'S INTENTIONS

REMINDER TO:

QUOTE FOR TODAY

INSPIRED THOUGHTS :

TODAY'S PRIORITIES:

EXERCISE:

TOTAL MINUTES:	
TOTAL STEPS:	

WATER INTAKE:

○ ○ ○ ○ ○ ○ ○

MEAL TRACKER:

BREAKFAST:	LUNCH:
DINNER:	SNACKS:

TO CALL OR EMAIL:

MONEY

MANIFESTED:	GRATEFULLY OUT:

TODAY I AM GRATEFUL FOR:

NOTES:

NEXT DAY GET AHEAD

DAILY LIFE MAGIC

DATE:

(S) (M) (T) (W) (T) (F) (S)

JOY LEVEL

TODAY'S INTENTIONS

REMINDER TO:

QUOTE FOR TODAY

INSPIRED THOUGHTS :

TODAY'S PRIORITES:

EXERCISE:

TOTAL MINUTES:	
TOTAL STEPS:	

WATER INTAKE:

MEAL TRACKER:

TO CALL OR EMAIL:

MONEY

BREAKFAST:	LUNCH:
DINNER:	SNACKS:

MANIFESTED:	GRATEFULLY OUT:

TODAY I AM GRATEFUL FOR:

NOTES:

NEXT DAY GET AHEAD

DAILY LIFE MAGIC

DATE:
(S) (M) (T) (W) (T) (F) (S)

JOY LEVEL

TODAY'S INTENTIONS

REMINDER TO:

QUOTE FOR TODAY

INSPIRED THOUGHTS :

TODAY'S PRIORITES:

EXERCISE:

TOTAL MINUTES:	
TOTAL STEPS:	

WATER INTAKE:

MEAL TRACKER:

BREAKFAST:	LUNCH:
DINNER:	SNACKS:

TO CALL OR EMAIL:

MONEY

MANIFESTED:	GRATEFULLY OUT:

TODAY I AM GRATEFUL FOR:

NOTES:

NEXT DAY GET AHEAD

DAILY LIFE MAGIC

DATE:
Ⓢ Ⓜ Ⓣ Ⓦ Ⓣ Ⓕ Ⓢ

JOY LEVEL

TODAY'S INTENTIONS

REMINDER TO:

QUOTE FOR TODAY

INSPIRED THOUGHTS:

TODAY'S PRIORITES:

EXERCISE:

TOTAL MINUTES:	
TOTAL STEPS:	

WATER INTAKE:
◊ ◊ ◊ ◊ ◊ ◊ ◊

MEAL TRACKER:

BREAKFAST:	LUNCH:
DINNER:	SNACKS:

TO CALL OR EMAIL:

MONEY

MANIFESTED:	GRATEFULLY OUT:

TODAY I AM GRATEFUL FOR:

NOTES:

NEXT DAY GET AHEAD

DAILY LIFE MAGIC

DATE:
(S) (M) (T) (W) (T) (F) (S)

JOY LEVEL

QUOTE FOR TODAY

TODAY'S INTENTIONS

REMINDER TO:

EXERCISE:

TOTAL MINUTES:	
TOTAL STEPS:	

WATER INTAKE:

○ ○ ○ ○ ○ ○ ○

MEAL TRACKER:

BREAKFAST:	LUNCH:
DINNER:	SNACKS:

TODAY'S PRIORITIES:

TO CALL OR EMAIL:

NOTES:

INSPIRED THOUGHTS:

MONEY

MANIFESTED:	GRATEFULLY OUT:

NEXT DAY GET AHEAD

TODAY I AM GRATEFUL FOR:

DAILY LIFE MAGIC

DATE:

JOY LEVEL

TODAY'S INTENTIONS

REMINDER TO:

QUOTE FOR TODAY

INSPIRED THOUGHTS:

TODAY'S PRIORITES:

EXERCISE:

TOTAL MINUTES:	
TOTAL STEPS:	

WATER INTAKE:

◊ ◊ ◊ ◊ ◊ ◊

MEAL TRACKER:

BREAKFAST:	LUNCH:
DINNER:	SNACKS:

TO CALL OR EMAIL:

MONEY

MANIFESTED:	GRATEFULLY OUT:

TODAY I AM GRATEFUL FOR:

NOTES:

NEXT DAY GET AHEAD

DAILY LIFE MAGIC

DATE:
(S) (M) (T) (W) (T) (F) (S)

JOY LEVEL

TODAY'S INTENTIONS

REMINDER TO:

QUOTE FOR TODAY

INSPIRED THOUGHTS :

TODAY'S PRIORITES:

EXERCISE:

TOTAL MINUTES:	
TOTAL STEPS:	

WATER INTAKE:

MEAL TRACKER:

BREAKFAST:	LUNCH:
DINNER:	SNACKS:

TO CALL OR EMAIL:

MONEY

MANIFESTED:	GRATEFULLY OUT:

TODAY I AM GRATEFUL FOR:

NOTES:

NEXT DAY GET AHEAD

DAILY LIFE MAGIC

DATE:

S M T W T F S

JOY LEVEL

TODAY'S INTENTIONS

REMINDER TO:

QUOTE FOR TODAY

INSPIRED THOUGHTS:

TODAY'S PRIORITES:

EXERCISE:

TOTAL MINUTES:	
TOTAL STEPS:	

WATER INTAKE:

○ ○ ○ ○ ○ ○ ○

MEAL TRACKER:

BREAKFAST:	LUNCH:
DINNER:	SNACKS:

TO CALL OR EMAIL:

MONEY

MANIFESTED:	GRATEFULLY OUT:

TODAY I AM GRATEFUL FOR:

NOTES:

NEXT DAY GET AHEAD

DAILY LIFE MAGIC

DATE:
Ⓢ Ⓜ Ⓣ Ⓦ Ⓣ Ⓕ Ⓢ

JOY LEVEL

TODAY'S INTENTIONS

REMINDER TO:

QUOTE FOR TODAY

INSPIRED THOUGHTS :

TODAY'S PRIORITES:

EXERCISE:

TOTAL MINUTES:	
TOTAL STEPS:	

WATER INTAKE:

MEAL TRACKER:

BREAKFAST:	LUNCH:
DINNER:	SNACKS:

TO CALL OR EMAIL:

MONEY

MANIFESTED:	GRATEFULLY OUT:

TODAY I AM GRATEFUL FOR:

NOTES:

NEXT DAY GET AHEAD

DAILY LIFE MAGIC

DATE:
(S) (M) (T) (W) (T) (F) (S)

JOY LEVEL

QUOTE FOR TODAY

TODAY'S INTENTIONS

REMINDER TO:

INSPIRED THOUGHTS:

TODAY'S PRIORITES:

EXERCISE:

TOTAL MINUTES:	
TOTAL STEPS:	

WATER INTAKE:
◯ ◯ ◯ ◯ ◯ ◯ ◯

MEAL TRACKER:

BREAKFAST:	LUNCH:
DINNER:	SNACKS:

TO CALL OR EMAIL:

MONEY

MANIFESTED:	GRATEFULLY OUT:

TODAY I AM GRATEFUL FOR:

NOTES:

NEXT DAY GET AHEAD

DAILY LIFE MAGIC

DATE:
Ⓢ Ⓜ Ⓣ Ⓦ Ⓣ Ⓕ Ⓢ

JOY LEVEL

TODAY'S INTENTIONS

REMINDER TO:

QUOTE FOR TODAY

INSPIRED THOUGHTS :

TODAY'S PRIORITES:

EXERCISE:

TOTAL MINUTES:	
TOTAL STEPS:	

WATER INTAKE:

MEAL TRACKER:

TO CALL OR EMAIL:

MONEY

BREAKFAST:	LUNCH:
DINNER:	SNACKS:

MANIFESTED:	GRATEFULLY OUT:

TODAY I AM GRATEFUL FOR:

NOTES:

NEXT DAY GET AHEAD

DAILY LIFE MAGIC

DATE:
 S M T W T F S

JOY LEVEL

TODAY'S INTENTIONS

REMINDER TO:

QUOTE FOR TODAY

INSPIRED THOUGHTS:

TODAY'S PRIORITES:

EXERCISE:

TOTAL MINUTES:	
TOTAL STEPS:	

WATER INTAKE:

MEAL TRACKER:

TO CALL OR EMAIL:

MONEY

BREAKFAST:	LUNCH:
DINNER:	SNACKS:

MANIFESTED:	GRATEFULLY OUT:

TODAY I AM GRATEFUL FOR:

NOTES:

NEXT DAY GET AHEAD

DAILY LIFE MAGIC

DATE:
(S) (M) (T) (W) (T) (F) (S)

JOY LEVEL

TODAY'S INTENTIONS

REMINDER TO:

QUOTE FOR TODAY

EXERCISE:

TOTAL MINUTES:	
TOTAL STEPS:	

WATER INTAKE:

MEAL TRACKER:

BREAKFAST:	LUNCH:
DINNER:	SNACKS:

TODAY'S PRIORITES:

TO CALL OR EMAIL:

INSPIRED THOUGHTS:

MONEY

MANIFESTED:	GRATEFULLY OUT:

TODAY I AM GRATEFUL FOR:

NOTES:

NEXT DAY GET AHEAD

DAILY LIFE MAGIC

DATE:

JOY LEVEL

TODAY'S INTENTIONS

REMINDER TO:

QUOTE FOR TODAY

INSPIRED THOUGHTS :

TODAY'S PRIORITES:

EXERCISE:

TOTAL MINUTES:	
TOTAL STEPS:	

WATER INTAKE:

MEAL TRACKER:

BREAKFAST:	LUNCH:
DINNER:	SNACKS:

TO CALL OR EMAIL:

MONEY

MANIFESTED:	GRATEFULLY OUT:

TODAY I AM GRATEFUL FOR:

NOTES:

NEXT DAY GET AHEAD

DAILY LIFE MAGIC

DATE:
(S) (M) (T) (W) (T) (F) (S)

JOY LEVEL

TODAY'S INTENTIONS

REMINDER TO:

QUOTE FOR TODAY

TODAY'S PRIORITES:

INSPIRED THOUGHTS:

EXERCISE:

TOTAL MINUTES:	
TOTAL STEPS:	

WATER INTAKE:

MEAL TRACKER:

BREAKFAST:	LUNCH:
DINNER:	SNACKS:

TO CALL OR EMAIL:

MONEY

MANIFESTED:	GRATEFULLY OUT:

TODAY I AM GRATEFUL FOR:

NOTES:

NEXT DAY GET AHEAD

DAILY LIFE MAGIC

DATE:
Ⓢ Ⓜ Ⓣ Ⓦ Ⓣ Ⓕ Ⓢ

JOY LEVEL

TODAY'S INTENTIONS

REMINDER TO:

QUOTE FOR TODAY

INSPIRED THOUGHTS :

TODAY'S PRIORITES:

EXERCISE:

TOTAL MINUTES:	
TOTAL STEPS:	

WATER INTAKE:

○ ○ ○ ○ ○ ○ ○

MEAL TRACKER:

BREAKFAST:	LUNCH:
DINNER:	SNACKS:

TO CALL OR EMAIL:

MONEY

MANIFESTED:	GRATEFULLY OUT:

TODAY I AM GRATEFUL FOR:

NOTES:

NEXT DAY GET AHEAD

DAILY LIFE MAGIC

DATE:
(S) (M) (T) (W) (T) (F) (S)

JOY LEVEL

TODAY'S INTENTIONS

REMINDER TO:

QUOTE FOR TODAY

INSPIRED THOUGHTS:

TODAY'S PRIORITIES:

EXERCISE:

TOTAL MINUTES:	
TOTAL STEPS:	

WATER INTAKE:

MEAL TRACKER:

BREAKFAST:	LUNCH:
DINNER:	SNACKS:

TO CALL OR EMAIL:

MONEY

MANIFESTED:	GRATEFULLY OUT:

TODAY I AM GRATEFUL FOR:

NOTES:

NEXT DAY GET AHEAD

DAILY LIFE MAGIC

DATE:

JOY LEVEL

TODAY'S INTENTIONS

REMINDER TO:

QUOTE FOR TODAY

INSPIRED THOUGHTS:

TODAY'S PRIORITES:

EXERCISE:

TOTAL MINUTES:	
TOTAL STEPS:	

WATER INTAKE:

◊ ◊ ◊ ◊ ◊ ◊ ◊

MEAL TRACKER:

BREAKFAST:	LUNCH:
DINNER:	SNACKS:

TO CALL OR EMAIL:

MONEY

MANIFESTED:	GRATEFULLY OUT:

TODAY I AM GRATEFUL FOR:

NOTES:

NEXT DAY GET AHEAD

DAILY LIFE MAGIC

DATE:
(S) (M) (T) (W) (T) (F) (S)

JOY LEVEL

TODAY'S INTENTIONS

REMINDER TO:

QUOTE FOR TODAY

INSPIRED THOUGHTS :

EXERCISE:

TOTAL MINUTES:	
TOTAL STEPS:	

TODAY'S PRIORITES:

WATER INTAKE:

MEAL TRACKER:

BREAKFAST:	LUNCH:
DINNER:	SNACKS:

TO CALL OR EMAIL:

MONEY

MANIFESTED:	GRATEFULLY OUT:

TODAY I AM GRATEFUL FOR:

NOTES:

NEXT DAY GET AHEAD

DAILY LIFE MAGIC

DATE:

JOY LEVEL

TODAY'S INTENTIONS

REMINDER TO:

QUOTE FOR TODAY

INSPIRED THOUGHTS :

TODAY'S PRIORITES:

EXERCISE:

TOTAL MINUTES:	
TOTAL STEPS:	

WATER INTAKE:

MEAL TRACKER:

BREAKFAST:	LUNCH:
DINNER:	SNACKS:

TO CALL OR EMAIL:

MONEY

MANIFESTED:	GRATEFULLY OUT:

TODAY I AM GRATEFUL FOR:

NOTES:

NEXT DAY GET AHEAD

DAILY LIFE MAGIC

DATE:
Ⓢ Ⓜ Ⓣ Ⓦ Ⓣ Ⓕ Ⓢ

JOY LEVEL

😊 🙂 😐 🙁 😢

QUOTE FOR TODAY

TODAY'S INTENTIONS

REMINDER TO:

INSPIRED THOUGHTS:

TODAY'S PRIORITES:

EXERCISE:

TOTAL MINUTES:	
TOTAL STEPS:	

WATER INTAKE:
💧💧💧💧💧💧💧

MEAL TRACKER:

BREAKFAST:	LUNCH:
DINNER:	SNACKS:

TO CALL OR EMAIL:

MONEY

MANIFESTED:	GRATEFULLY OUT:

TODAY I AM GRATEFUL FOR:

NOTES:

NEXT DAY GET AHEAD

DAILY LIFE MAGIC

DATE:
Ⓢ Ⓜ Ⓣ Ⓦ Ⓣ Ⓕ Ⓢ

JOY LEVEL

TODAY'S INTENTIONS

REMINDER TO:

QUOTE FOR TODAY

INSPIRED THOUGHTS:

TODAY'S PRIORITES:

EXERCISE:

TOTAL MINUTES:	
TOTAL STEPS:	

WATER INTAKE:
○ ○ ○ ○ ○ ○ ○

MEAL TRACKER:

BREAKFAST:	LUNCH:
DINNER:	SNACKS:

TO CALL OR EMAIL:

MONEY

MANIFESTED:	GRATEFULLY OUT:

TODAY I AM GRATEFUL FOR:

NOTES:

NEXT DAY GET AHEAD

DAILY LIFE MAGIC

DATE:
(S) (M) (T) (W) (T) (F) (S)

JOY LEVEL

TODAY'S INTENTIONS

REMINDER TO:

QUOTE FOR TODAY

INSPIRED THOUGHTS:

TODAY'S PRIORITIES:

EXERCISE:

TOTAL MINUTES:	
TOTAL STEPS:	

WATER INTAKE:

MEAL TRACKER:

TO CALL OR EMAIL:

MONEY

BREAKFAST:	LUNCH:
DINNER:	SNACKS:

MANIFESTED:	GRATEFULLY OUT:

TODAY I AM GRATEFUL FOR:

NOTES:

NEXT DAY GET AHEAD

DAILY LIFE MAGIC

DATE:

JOY LEVEL

TODAY'S INTENTIONS

REMINDER TO:

QUOTE FOR TODAY

INSPIRED THOUGHTS :

TODAY'S PRIORITES:

EXERCISE:

TOTAL MINUTES:	
TOTAL STEPS:	

WATER INTAKE:
◯ ◯ ◯ ◯ ◯ ◯ ◯

MEAL TRACKER:

BREAKFAST:	LUNCH:
DINNER:	SNACKS:

TO CALL OR EMAIL:

MONEY

MANIFESTED:	GRATEFULLY OUT:

TODAY I AM GRATEFUL FOR:

NOTES:

NEXT DAY GET AHEAD

DAILY LIFE MAGIC

DATE:
Ⓢ Ⓜ Ⓣ Ⓦ Ⓣ Ⓕ Ⓢ

JOY LEVEL

TODAY'S INTENTIONS

REMINDER TO:

QUOTE FOR TODAY

TODAY'S PRIORITES:

INSPIRED THOUGHTS :

EXERCISE:

TOTAL MINUTES:	
TOTAL STEPS:	

WATER INTAKE:

MEAL TRACKER:

BREAKFAST:	LUNCH:
DINNER:	SNACKS:

TO CALL OR EMAIL:

MONEY

MANIFESTED:	GRATEFULLY OUT:

TODAY I AM GRATEFUL FOR:

NOTES:

NEXT DAY GET AHEAD

DAILY LIFE MAGIC

DATE:

JOY LEVEL

TODAY'S INTENTIONS

REMINDER TO:

QUOTE FOR TODAY

INSPIRED THOUGHTS :

TODAY'S PRIORITES:

EXERCISE:

TOTAL MINUTES:	
TOTAL STEPS:	

WATER INTAKE:

MEAL TRACKER:

BREAKFAST:	LUNCH:
DINNER:	SNACKS:

TO CALL OR EMAIL:

MONEY

MANIFESTED:	GRATEFULLY OUT:

TODAY I AM GRATEFUL FOR:

NOTES:

NEXT DAY GET AHEAD

DAILY LIFE MAGIC

DATE:

Ⓢ Ⓜ Ⓣ Ⓦ Ⓣ Ⓕ Ⓢ

JOY LEVEL

TODAY'S INTENTIONS

REMINDER TO:

QUOTE FOR TODAY

INSPIRED THOUGHTS:

TODAY'S PRIORITIES:

EXERCISE:

TOTAL MINUTES:	
TOTAL STEPS:	

WATER INTAKE:

MEAL TRACKER:

BREAKFAST:	LUNCH:
DINNER:	SNACKS:

TO CALL OR EMAIL:

MONEY

MANIFESTED:	GRATEFULLY OUT:

TODAY I AM GRATEFUL FOR:

NOTES:

NEXT DAY GET AHEAD

DAILY LIFE MAGIC

DATE:
Ⓢ Ⓜ Ⓣ Ⓦ Ⓣ Ⓕ Ⓢ

JOY LEVEL

TODAY'S INTENTIONS

REMINDER TO:

QUOTE FOR TODAY

INSPIRED THOUGHTS :

TODAY'S PRIORITIES:

EXERCISE:

TOTAL MINUTES:	
TOTAL STEPS:	

WATER INTAKE:
💧💧💧💧💧💧💧💧

MEAL TRACKER:

BREAKFAST:	LUNCH:
DINNER:	SNACKS:

TO CALL OR EMAIL:

MONEY

MANIFESTED:	GRATEFULLY OUT:

TODAY I AM GRATEFUL FOR:

NOTES:

NEXT DAY GET AHEAD

DAILY LIFE MAGIC

DATE:

(S) (M) (T) (W) (T) (F) (S)

JOY LEVEL

TODAY'S INTENTIONS

REMINDER TO:

QUOTE FOR TODAY

INSPIRED THOUGHTS :

TODAY'S PRIORITIES:

EXERCISE:

TOTAL MINUTES:	
TOTAL STEPS:	

WATER INTAKE:

MEAL TRACKER:

BREAKFAST:	LUNCH:
DINNER:	SNACKS:

TO CALL OR EMAIL:

MONEY

MANIFESTED:	GRATEFULLY OUT:

TODAY I AM GRATEFUL FOR:

NOTES:

NEXT DAY GET AHEAD

DAILY LIFE MAGIC

DATE:
(S) (M) (T) (W) (T) (F) (S)

JOY LEVEL

TODAY'S INTENTIONS

REMINDER TO:

QUOTE FOR TODAY

TODAY'S PRIORITES:

INSPIRED THOUGHTS:

EXERCISE:

TOTAL MINUTES:	
TOTAL STEPS:	

WATER INTAKE:

MEAL TRACKER:

BREAKFAST:	LUNCH:
DINNER:	SNACKS:

TO CALL OR EMAIL:

MONEY

MANIFESTED:	GRATEFULLY OUT:

TODAY I AM GRATEFUL FOR:

NOTES:

NEXT DAY GET AHEAD

DAILY LIFE MAGIC

DATE:

Ⓢ Ⓜ Ⓣ Ⓦ Ⓣ Ⓕ Ⓢ

JOY LEVEL

😁 🙂 😐 🙁 😢

QUOTE FOR TODAY

TODAY'S INTENTIONS

REMINDER TO:

INSPIRED THOUGHTS:

TODAY'S PRIORITES:

EXERCISE:

TOTAL MINUTES:	
TOTAL STEPS:	

WATER INTAKE:

💧 💧 💧 💧 💧 💧 💧

MEAL TRACKER:

BREAKFAST:	LUNCH:
DINNER:	SNACKS:

TO CALL OR EMAIL:

MONEY

MANIFESTED:	GRATEFULLY OUT:

TODAY I AM GRATEFUL FOR:

NOTES:

NEXT DAY GET AHEAD

DAILY LIFE MAGIC

DATE:

(S) (M) (T) (W) (T) (F) (S)

JOY LEVEL

TODAY'S INTENTIONS

REMINDER TO:

QUOTE FOR TODAY

INSPIRED THOUGHTS:

TODAY'S PRIORITES:

EXERCISE:

TOTAL MINUTES:	
TOTAL STEPS:	

WATER INTAKE:

MEAL TRACKER:

TO CALL OR EMAIL:

MONEY

BREAKFAST:	LUNCH:
DINNER:	SNACKS:

MANIFESTED:	GRATEFULLY OUT:

TODAY I AM GRATEFUL FOR:

NOTES:

NEXT DAY GET AHEAD

DAILY LIFE MAGIC

DATE:

(S) (M) (T) (W) (T) (F) (S)

JOY LEVEL

TODAY'S INTENTIONS

REMINDER TO:

QUOTE FOR TODAY

TODAY'S PRIORITES:

INSPIRED THOUGHTS :

EXERCISE:

TOTAL MINUTES:	
TOTAL STEPS:	

WATER INTAKE:

◯ ◯ ◯ ◯ ◯ ◯

MEAL TRACKER:

BREAKFAST:	LUNCH:
DINNER:	SNACKS:

TO CALL OR EMAIL:

MONEY

MANIFESTED:	GRATEFULLY OUT:

TODAY I AM GRATEFUL FOR:

NOTES:

NEXT DAY GET AHEAD

DAILY LIFE MAGIC

DATE:

Ⓢ Ⓜ Ⓣ Ⓦ Ⓣ Ⓕ Ⓢ

JOY LEVEL

😃 🙂 😐 🙁 😢

QUOTE FOR TODAY

TODAY'S INTENTIONS

REMINDER TO:

INSPIRED THOUGHTS :

TODAY'S PRIORITES:

EXERCISE:

TOTAL MINUTES:	
TOTAL STEPS:	

WATER INTAKE:

💧 💧 💧 💧 💧 💧 💧

MEAL TRACKER:

BREAKFAST:	LUNCH:
DINNER:	SNACKS:

TO CALL OR EMAIL:

MONEY

MANIFESTED:	GRATEFULLY OUT:

TODAY I AM GRATEFUL FOR:

NOTES:

NEXT DAY GET AHEAD

DAILY LIFE MAGIC

DATE:

(S) (M) (T) (W) (T) (F) (S)

JOY LEVEL

TODAY'S INTENTIONS

REMINDER TO:

QUOTE FOR TODAY

INSPIRED THOUGHTS :

TODAY'S PRIORITES:

EXERCISE:

TOTAL MINUTES:	
TOTAL STEPS:	

WATER INTAKE:

MEAL TRACKER:

BREAKFAST:	LUNCH:
DINNER:	SNACKS:

TO CALL OR EMAIL:

MONEY

MANIFESTED:	GRATEFULLY OUT:

TODAY I AM GRATEFUL FOR:

NOTES:

NEXT DAY GET AHEAD

DAILY LIFE MAGIC

DATE:
Ⓢ Ⓜ Ⓣ Ⓦ Ⓣ Ⓕ Ⓢ

JOY LEVEL

TODAY'S INTENTIONS

REMINDER TO:

QUOTE FOR TODAY

TODAY'S PRIORITES:

INSPIRED THOUGHTS:

EXERCISE:

TOTAL MINUTES:	
TOTAL STEPS:	

WATER INTAKE:

◯ ◯ ◯ ◯ ◯ ◯

MEAL TRACKER:

BREAKFAST:	LUNCH:
DINNER:	SNACKS:

TO CALL OR EMAIL:

MONEY

MANIFESTED:	GRATEFULLY OUT:

TODAY I AM GRATEFUL FOR:

NOTES:

NEXT DAY GET AHEAD

DAILY LIFE MAGIC

DATE:

(S) (M) (T) (W) (T) (F) (S)

JOY LEVEL

TODAY'S INTENTIONS

REMINDER TO:

QUOTE FOR TODAY

EXERCISE:

TOTAL MINUTES:	
TOTAL STEPS:	

WATER INTAKE:

◯ ◯ ◯ ◯ ◯ ◯ ◯

MEAL TRACKER:

BREAKFAST:	LUNCH:
DINNER:	SNACKS:

TODAY'S PRIORITES:

TO CALL OR EMAIL:

INSPIRED THOUGHTS :

MONEY

MANIFESTED:	GRATEFULLY OUT:

TODAY I AM GRATEFUL FOR:

NOTES:

NEXT DAY GET AHEAD

DAILY LIFE MAGIC

DATE:
S M T W T F S

JOY LEVEL

TODAY'S INTENTIONS

REMINDER TO:

QUOTE FOR TODAY

INSPIRED THOUGHTS:

TODAY'S PRIORITES:

EXERCISE:

TOTAL MINUTES:	
TOTAL STEPS:	

WATER INTAKE:

MEAL TRACKER:

BREAKFAST:	LUNCH:
DINNER:	SNACKS:

TO CALL OR EMAIL:

MONEY

MANIFESTED:	GRATEFULLY OUT:

TODAY I AM GRATEFUL FOR:

NOTES:

NEXT DAY GET AHEAD

DAILY LIFE MAGIC

DATE:

Ⓢ Ⓜ Ⓣ Ⓦ Ⓣ Ⓕ Ⓢ

JOY LEVEL

TODAY'S INTENTIONS

REMINDER TO:

QUOTE FOR TODAY

INSPIRED THOUGHTS :

TODAY'S PRIORITES:

EXERCISE:

TOTAL MINUTES:	
TOTAL STEPS:	

WATER INTAKE:

💧💧💧💧💧💧💧

MEAL TRACKER:

BREAKFAST:	LUNCH:
DINNER:	SNACKS:

TO CALL OR EMAIL:

MONEY

MANIFESTED:	GRATEFULLY OUT:

TODAY I AM GRATEFUL FOR:

NOTES:

NEXT DAY GET AHEAD

DAILY LIFE MAGIC

DATE:

Ⓢ Ⓜ Ⓣ Ⓦ Ⓣ Ⓕ Ⓢ

JOY LEVEL

😃 🙂 😐 🙁 😢

TODAY'S INTENTIONS

REMINDER TO:

QUOTE FOR TODAY

INSPIRED THOUGHTS :

TODAY'S PRIORITES:

EXERCISE:

TOTAL MINUTES:	
TOTAL STEPS:	

WATER INTAKE:

💧 💧 💧 💧 💧 💧 💧

MEAL TRACKER:

BREAKFAST:	LUNCH:
DINNER:	SNACKS:

TO CALL OR EMAIL:

MONEY

MANIFESTED:	GRATEFULLY OUT:

TODAY I AM GRATEFUL FOR:

NOTES:

NEXT DAY GET AHEAD

DAILY LIFE MAGIC

DATE:
(S) (M) (T) (W) (T) (F) (S)

JOY LEVEL

TODAY'S INTENTIONS

REMINDER TO:

QUOTE FOR TODAY

INSPIRED THOUGHTS:

TODAY'S PRIORITES:

EXERCISE:

TOTAL MINUTES:	
TOTAL STEPS:	

WATER INTAKE:

MEAL TRACKER:

BREAKFAST:	LUNCH:
DINNER:	SNACKS:

TO CALL OR EMAIL:

MONEY

MANIFESTED:	GRATEFULLY OUT:

TODAY I AM GRATEFUL FOR:

NOTES:

NEXT DAY GET AHEAD

DAILY LIFE MAGIC

DATE:

S M T W T F S

JOY LEVEL

TODAY'S INTENTIONS

REMINDER TO:

QUOTE FOR TODAY

INSPIRED THOUGHTS:

TODAY'S PRIORITES:

EXERCISE:

TOTAL MINUTES:	
TOTAL STEPS:	

WATER INTAKE:

MEAL TRACKER:

TO CALL OR EMAIL:

MONEY

BREAKFAST:	LUNCH:
DINNER:	SNACKS:

MANIFESTED:	GRATEFULLY OUT:

TODAY I AM GRATEFUL FOR:

NOTES:

NEXT DAY GET AHEAD

DAILY LIFE MAGIC

DATE:

(S) (M) (T) (W) (T) (F) (S)

JOY LEVEL

TODAY'S INTENTIONS

REMINDER TO:

QUOTE FOR TODAY

EXERCISE:

TOTAL MINUTES:	
TOTAL STEPS:	

WATER INTAKE:

○ ○ ○ ○ ○ ○ ○

MEAL TRACKER:

BREAKFAST:	LUNCH:
DINNER:	SNACKS:

TODAY'S PRIORITES:

TO CALL OR EMAIL:

NOTES:

INSPIRED THOUGHTS :

MONEY

MANIFESTED:	GRATEFULLY OUT:

NEXT DAY GET AHEAD

TODAY I AM GRATEFUL FOR:

DAILY LIFE MAGIC

DATE:
Ⓢ Ⓜ Ⓣ Ⓦ Ⓣ Ⓕ Ⓢ

JOY LEVEL

TODAY'S INTENTIONS

REMINDER TO:

QUOTE FOR TODAY

INSPIRED THOUGHTS :

TODAY'S PRIORITES:

EXERCISE:

TOTAL MINUTES:	
TOTAL STEPS:	

WATER INTAKE:

○ ○ ○ ○ ○ ○ ○

MEAL TRACKER:

BREAKFAST:	LUNCH:
DINNER:	SNACKS:

TO CALL OR EMAIL:

MONEY

MANIFESTED:	GRATEFULLY OUT:

TODAY I AM GRATEFUL FOR:

NOTES:

NEXT DAY GET AHEAD

DAILY LIFE MAGIC

DATE:
(S) (M) (T) (W) (T) (F) (S)

JOY LEVEL

😊 🙂 😐 🙁 😢

QUOTE FOR TODAY

TODAY'S INTENTIONS

REMINDER TO:

INSPIRED THOUGHTS:

TODAY'S PRIORITIES:

EXERCISE:

TOTAL MINUTES:	
TOTAL STEPS:	

WATER INTAKE:

💧 💧 💧 💧 💧 💧 💧

MEAL TRACKER:

BREAKFAST:	LUNCH:
DINNER:	SNACKS:

TO CALL OR EMAIL:

MONEY

MANIFESTED:	GRATEFULLY OUT:

TODAY I AM GRATEFUL FOR:

NOTES:

NEXT DAY GET AHEAD

DAILY LIFE MAGIC

DATE:

(S) (M) (T) (W) (T) (F) (S)

JOY LEVEL

TODAY'S INTENTIONS

REMINDER TO:

QUOTE FOR TODAY

TODAY'S PRIORITIES:

INSPIRED THOUGHTS:

EXERCISE:

TOTAL MINUTES:	
TOTAL STEPS:	

WATER INTAKE:

MEAL TRACKER:

BREAKFAST:	LUNCH:
DINNER:	SNACKS:

TO CALL OR EMAIL:

MONEY

MANIFESTED:	GRATEFULLY OUT:

TODAY I AM GRATEFUL FOR:

NOTES:

NEXT DAY GET AHEAD

DAILY LIFE MAGIC

DATE:
(S) (M) (T) (W) (T) (F) (S)

JOY LEVEL

QUOTE FOR TODAY

TODAY'S INTENTIONS

REMINDER TO:

INSPIRED THOUGHTS :

TODAY'S PRIORITES:

EXERCISE:

TOTAL MINUTES:	
TOTAL STEPS:	

WATER INTAKE:

MEAL TRACKER:

BREAKFAST:	LUNCH:
DINNER:	SNACKS:

TO CALL OR EMAIL:

MONEY

MANIFESTED:	GRATEFULLY OUT:

TODAY I AM GRATEFUL FOR:

NOTES:

NEXT DAY GET AHEAD

DAILY LIFE MAGIC

DATE:
Ⓢ Ⓜ Ⓣ Ⓦ Ⓣ Ⓕ Ⓢ

JOY LEVEL

TODAY'S INTENTIONS

REMINDER TO:

QUOTE FOR TODAY

INSPIRED THOUGHTS :

TODAY'S PRIORITES:

EXERCISE:

TOTAL MINUTES:	
TOTAL STEPS:	

WATER INTAKE:

MEAL TRACKER:

TO CALL OR EMAIL:

MONEY

BREAKFAST:	LUNCH:
DINNER:	SNACKS:

MANIFESTED:	GRATEFULLY OUT:

TODAY I AM GRATEFUL FOR:

NOTES:

NEXT DAY GET AHEAD

DAILY LIFE MAGIC

DATE:

(S) (M) (T) (W) (T) (F) (S)

JOY LEVEL

TODAY'S INTENTIONS

REMINDER TO:

QUOTE FOR TODAY

INSPIRED THOUGHTS:

TODAY'S PRIORITES:

EXERCISE:

TOTAL MINUTES:	
TOTAL STEPS:	

WATER INTAKE:

MEAL TRACKER:

BREAKFAST:	LUNCH:
DINNER:	SNACKS:

TO CALL OR EMAIL:

MONEY

MANIFESTED:	GRATEFULLY OUT:

TODAY I AM GRATEFUL FOR:

NOTES:

NEXT DAY GET AHEAD

DAILY LIFE MAGIC

DATE:
Ⓢ Ⓜ Ⓣ Ⓦ Ⓣ Ⓕ Ⓢ

JOY LEVEL

TODAY'S INTENTIONS

REMINDER TO:

QUOTE FOR TODAY

INSPIRED THOUGHTS :

TODAY'S PRIORITES:

EXERCISE:

TOTAL MINUTES:	
TOTAL STEPS:	

WATER INTAKE:

💧💧💧💧💧💧

MEAL TRACKER:

BREAKFAST:	LUNCH:
DINNER:	SNACKS:

TO CALL OR EMAIL:

MONEY

MANIFESTED:	GRATEFULLY OUT:

TODAY I AM GRATEFUL FOR:

NOTES:

NEXT DAY GET AHEAD

DAILY LIFE MAGIC

DATE:
(S) (M) (T) (W) (T) (F) (S)

JOY LEVEL

TODAY'S INTENTIONS

REMINDER TO:

QUOTE FOR TODAY

TODAY'S PRIORITES:

INSPIRED THOUGHTS:

EXERCISE:

TOTAL MINUTES:	
TOTAL STEPS:	

WATER INTAKE:

MEAL TRACKER:

BREAKFAST:	LUNCH:
DINNER:	SNACKS:

TO CALL OR EMAIL:

MONEY

MANIFESTED:	GRATEFULLY OUT:

TODAY I AM GRATEFUL FOR:

NOTES:

NEXT DAY GET AHEAD

DAILY LIFE MAGIC

DATE:

Ⓢ Ⓜ Ⓣ Ⓦ Ⓣ Ⓕ Ⓢ

JOY LEVEL

😃 🙂 😐 🙁 😢

TODAY'S INTENTIONS

REMINDER TO:

QUOTE FOR TODAY

TODAY'S PRIORITIES:

INSPIRED THOUGHTS:

EXERCISE:

TOTAL MINUTES:	
TOTAL STEPS:	

WATER INTAKE:

💧💧💧💧💧💧💧

MEAL TRACKER:

BREAKFAST:	LUNCH:
DINNER:	SNACKS:

TO CALL OR EMAIL:

MONEY

MANIFESTED:	GRATEFULLY OUT:

TODAY I AM GRATEFUL FOR:

NOTES:

NEXT DAY GET AHEAD

DAILY LIFE MAGIC

DATE:
(S) (M) (T) (W) (T) (F) (S)

JOY LEVEL

TODAY'S INTENTIONS

REMINDER TO:

QUOTE FOR TODAY

INSPIRED THOUGHTS:

TODAY'S PRIORITIES:

EXERCISE:

TOTAL MINUTES:	
TOTAL STEPS:	

WATER INTAKE:
○ ○ ○ ○ ○ ○ ○

MEAL TRACKER:

BREAKFAST:	LUNCH:
DINNER:	SNACKS:

TO CALL OR EMAIL:

MONEY

MANIFESTED:	GRATEFULLY OUT:

TODAY I AM GRATEFUL FOR:

NOTES:

NEXT DAY GET AHEAD

DAILY LIFE MAGIC

DATE:

JOY LEVEL

TODAY'S INTENTIONS

REMINDER TO:

QUOTE FOR TODAY

INSPIRED THOUGHTS:

TODAY'S PRIORITES:

EXERCISE:

TOTAL MINUTES:	
TOTAL STEPS:	

WATER INTAKE:

MEAL TRACKER:

BREAKFAST:	LUNCH:
DINNER:	SNACKS:

TO CALL OR EMAIL:

MONEY

MANIFESTED:	GRATEFULLY OUT:

TODAY I AM GRATEFUL FOR:

NOTES:

NEXT DAY GET AHEAD

DAILY LIFE MAGIC

DATE:

(S) (M) (T) (W) (T) (F) (S)

JOY LEVEL

TODAY'S INTENTIONS

REMINDER TO:

QUOTE FOR TODAY

TODAY'S PRIORITES:

INSPIRED THOUGHTS :

EXERCISE:

TOTAL MINUTES:	
TOTAL STEPS:	

WATER INTAKE:

MEAL TRACKER:

BREAKFAST:	LUNCH:
DINNER:	SNACKS:

TO CALL OR EMAIL:

MONEY

MANIFESTED:	GRATEFULLY OUT:

TODAY I AM GRATEFUL FOR:

NOTES:

NEXT DAY GET AHEAD

DAILY LIFE MAGIC

DATE:

JOY LEVEL

TODAY'S INTENTIONS

REMINDER TO:

QUOTE FOR TODAY

INSPIRED THOUGHTS:

TODAY'S PRIORITES:

EXERCISE:

TOTAL MINUTES:	
TOTAL STEPS:	

WATER INTAKE:

○ ○ ○ ○ ○ ○ ○

MEAL TRACKER:

BREAKFAST:	LUNCH:
DINNER:	SNACKS:

TO CALL OR EMAIL:

MONEY

MANIFESTED:	GRATEFULLY OUT:

TODAY I AM GRATEFUL FOR:

NOTES:

NEXT DAY GET AHEAD

DAILY LIFE MAGIC

DATE:
Ⓢ Ⓜ Ⓣ Ⓦ Ⓣ Ⓕ Ⓢ

JOY LEVEL

😄 🙂 😐 🙁 😢

QUOTE FOR TODAY

TODAY'S INTENTIONS

REMINDER TO:

INSPIRED THOUGHTS:

TODAY'S PRIORITES:

EXERCISE:

TOTAL MINUTES:	
TOTAL STEPS:	

WATER INTAKE:

💧 💧 💧 💧 💧 💧

MEAL TRACKER:

BREAKFAST:	LUNCH:
DINNER:	SNACKS:

TO CALL OR EMAIL:

MONEY

MANIFESTED:	GRATEFULLY OUT:

TODAY I AM GRATEFUL FOR:

NOTES:

NEXT DAY GET AHEAD

DAILY LIFE MAGIC

DATE:

Ⓢ Ⓜ Ⓣ Ⓦ Ⓣ Ⓕ Ⓢ

JOY LEVEL

TODAY'S INTENTIONS

REMINDER TO:

QUOTE FOR TODAY

INSPIRED THOUGHTS :

TODAY'S PRIORITES:

EXERCISE:

TOTAL MINUTES:	
TOTAL STEPS:	

WATER INTAKE:

💧 💧 💧 💧 💧 💧

MEAL TRACKER:

BREAKFAST:	LUNCH:
DINNER:	SNACKS:

TO CALL OR EMAIL:

MONEY

MANIFESTED:	GRATEFULLY OUT:

TODAY I AM GRATEFUL FOR:

NOTES:

NEXT DAY GET AHEAD

DAILY LIFE MAGIC

DATE:
(S) (M) (T) (W) (T) (F) (S)

JOY LEVEL

TODAY'S INTENTIONS

REMINDER TO:

QUOTE FOR TODAY

INSPIRED THOUGHTS:

TODAY'S PRIORITIES:

EXERCISE:

TOTAL MINUTES:	
TOTAL STEPS:	

WATER INTAKE:
◊ ◊ ◊ ◊ ◊ ◊ ◊

MEAL TRACKER:

BREAKFAST:	LUNCH:
DINNER:	SNACKS:

TO CALL OR EMAIL:

MONEY

MANIFESTED:	GRATEFULLY OUT:

TODAY I AM GRATEFUL FOR:

NOTES:

NEXT DAY GET AHEAD

DAILY LIFE MAGIC

DATE:
Ⓢ Ⓜ Ⓣ Ⓦ Ⓣ Ⓕ Ⓢ

JOY LEVEL

TODAY'S INTENTIONS

REMINDER TO:

QUOTE FOR TODAY

INSPIRED THOUGHTS:

TODAY'S PRIORITES:

EXERCISE:

TOTAL MINUTES:	
TOTAL STEPS:	

WATER INTAKE:
◊ ◊ ◊ ◊ ◊ ◊ ◊

MEAL TRACKER:

BREAKFAST:	LUNCH:
DINNER:	SNACKS:

TO CALL OR EMAIL:

MONEY

MANIFESTED:	GRATEFULLY OUT:

TODAY I AM GRATEFUL FOR:

NOTES:

NEXT DAY GET AHEAD

DAILY LIFE MAGIC

DATE:

(S) (M) (T) (W) (T) (F) (S)

JOY LEVEL

TODAY'S INTENTIONS

REMINDER TO:

QUOTE FOR TODAY

EXERCISE:

TOTAL MINUTES:	
TOTAL STEPS:	

WATER INTAKE:

TODAY'S PRIORITES:

INSPIRED THOUGHTS:

MEAL TRACKER:

BREAKFAST:	LUNCH:
DINNER:	SNACKS:

TO CALL OR EMAIL:

MONEY

MANIFESTED:	GRATEFULLY OUT:

TODAY I AM GRATEFUL FOR:

NOTES:

NEXT DAY GET AHEAD

DAILY LIFE MAGIC

DATE:
S M T W T F S

JOY LEVEL

TODAY'S INTENTIONS

REMINDER TO:

QUOTE FOR TODAY

INSPIRED THOUGHTS :

TODAY'S PRIORITES:

EXERCISE:

TOTAL MINUTES:	
TOTAL STEPS:	

WATER INTAKE:

MEAL TRACKER:

BREAKFAST:	LUNCH:
DINNER:	SNACKS:

TO CALL OR EMAIL:

MONEY

MANIFESTED:	GRATEFULLY OUT:

TODAY I AM GRATEFUL FOR:

NOTES:

NEXT DAY GET AHEAD

DAILY LIFE MAGIC

DATE:

Ⓢ Ⓜ Ⓣ Ⓦ Ⓣ Ⓕ Ⓢ

JOY LEVEL

😀 🙂 😐 🙁 😢

QUOTE FOR TODAY

TODAY'S INTENTIONS

REMINDER TO:

INSPIRED THOUGHTS:

TODAY'S PRIORITES:

EXERCISE:

TOTAL MINUTES:	
TOTAL STEPS:	

WATER INTAKE:

💧💧💧💧💧💧

MEAL TRACKER:

BREAKFAST:	LUNCH:
DINNER:	SNACKS:

TO CALL OR EMAIL:

MONEY

MANIFESTED:	GRATEFULLY OUT:

TODAY I AM GRATEFUL FOR:

NOTES:

NEXT DAY GET AHEAD

DAILY LIFE MAGIC

DATE:

Ⓢ Ⓜ Ⓣ Ⓦ Ⓣ Ⓕ Ⓢ

JOY LEVEL

TODAY'S INTENTIONS

REMINDER TO:

QUOTE FOR TODAY

TODAY'S PRIORITES:

INSPIRED THOUGHTS :

EXERCISE:

TOTAL MINUTES:	
TOTAL STEPS:	

WATER INTAKE:

◊ ◊ ◊ ◊ ◊ ◊ ◊

MEAL TRACKER:

BREAKFAST:	LUNCH:
DINNER:	SNACKS:

TO CALL OR EMAIL:

MONEY

MANIFESTED:	GRATEFULLY OUT:

TODAY I AM GRATEFUL FOR:

NOTES:

NEXT DAY GET AHEAD

DAILY LIFE MAGIC

DATE:
(S) (M) (T) (W) (T) (F) (S)

JOY LEVEL

TODAY'S INTENTIONS

REMINDER TO:

QUOTE FOR TODAY

TODAY'S PRIORITIES:

INSPIRED THOUGHTS:

EXERCISE:

TOTAL MINUTES:	
TOTAL STEPS:	

WATER INTAKE:

MEAL TRACKER:

BREAKFAST:	LUNCH:
DINNER:	SNACKS:

TO CALL OR EMAIL:

MONEY

MANIFESTED:	GRATEFULLY OUT:

TODAY I AM GRATEFUL FOR:

NOTES:

NEXT DAY GET AHEAD

DAILY LIFE MAGIC

DATE:

(S) (M) (T) (W) (T) (F) (S)

JOY LEVEL

TODAY'S INTENTIONS

REMINDER TO:

QUOTE FOR TODAY

INSPIRED THOUGHTS :

TODAY'S PRIORITES:

EXERCISE:

TOTAL MINUTES:	
TOTAL STEPS:	

WATER INTAKE:

◊ ◊ ◊ ◊ ◊ ◊

MEAL TRACKER:

TO CALL OR EMAIL:

MONEY

BREAKFAST:	LUNCH:
DINNER:	SNACKS:

MANIFESTED:	GRATEFULLY OUT:

TODAY I AM GRATEFUL FOR:

NOTES:

NEXT DAY GET AHEAD

DAILY LIFE MAGIC

DATE:

(S) (M) (T) (W) (T) (F) (S)

JOY LEVEL

TODAY'S INTENTIONS

REMINDER TO:

QUOTE FOR TODAY

INSPIRED THOUGHTS:

TODAY'S PRIORITES:

EXERCISE:

TOTAL MINUTES:	
TOTAL STEPS:	

WATER INTAKE:

MEAL TRACKER:

BREAKFAST:	LUNCH:
DINNER:	SNACKS:

TO CALL OR EMAIL:

MONEY

MANIFESTED:	GRATEFULLY OUT:

TODAY I AM GRATEFUL FOR:

NOTES:

NEXT DAY GET AHEAD

DAILY LIFE MAGIC

DATE:

JOY LEVEL

TODAY'S INTENTIONS

REMINDER TO:

QUOTE FOR TODAY

INSPIRED THOUGHTS:

TODAY'S PRIORITES:

EXERCISE:

TOTAL MINUTES:	
TOTAL STEPS:	

WATER INTAKE:

MEAL TRACKER:

BREAKFAST:	LUNCH:
DINNER:	SNACKS:

TO CALL OR EMAIL:

MONEY

MANIFESTED:	GRATEFULLY OUT:

TODAY I AM GRATEFUL FOR:

NOTES:

NEXT DAY GET AHEAD

DAILY LIFE MAGIC

DATE:
Ⓢ Ⓜ Ⓣ Ⓦ Ⓣ Ⓕ Ⓢ

JOY LEVEL

TODAY'S INTENTIONS

REMINDER TO:

QUOTE FOR TODAY

INSPIRED THOUGHTS:

TODAY'S PRIORITES:

EXERCISE:

TOTAL MINUTES:	
TOTAL STEPS:	

WATER INTAKE:

○ ○ ○ ○ ○ ○ ○

MEAL TRACKER:

BREAKFAST:	LUNCH:
DINNER:	SNACKS:

TO CALL OR EMAIL:

MONEY

MANIFESTED:	GRATEFULLY OUT:

TODAY I AM GRATEFUL FOR:

NOTES:

NEXT DAY GET AHEAD

DAILY LIFE MAGIC

DATE:
(S) (M) (T) (W) (T) (F) (S)

JOY LEVEL

TODAY'S INTENTIONS

REMINDER TO:

QUOTE FOR TODAY

INSPIRED THOUGHTS :

TODAY'S PRIORITES:

EXERCISE:

TOTAL MINUTES:	
TOTAL STEPS:	

WATER INTAKE:

MEAL TRACKER:

TO CALL OR EMAIL:

MONEY

BREAKFAST:	LUNCH:
DINNER:	SNACKS:

MANIFESTED:	GRATEFULLY OUT:

TODAY I AM GRATEFUL FOR:

NOTES:

NEXT DAY GET AHEAD

DAILY LIFE MAGIC

DATE:
(S) (M) (T) (W) (T) (F) (S)

JOY LEVEL

QUOTE FOR TODAY

TODAY'S INTENTIONS

REMINDER TO:

INSPIRED THOUGHTS:

TODAY'S PRIORITES:

EXERCISE:

TOTAL MINUTES:	
TOTAL STEPS:	

WATER INTAKE:

MEAL TRACKER:

BREAKFAST:	LUNCH:
DINNER:	SNACKS:

TO CALL OR EMAIL:

MONEY

MANIFESTED:	GRATEFULLY OUT:

TODAY I AM GRATEFUL FOR:

NOTES:

NEXT DAY GET AHEAD

DAILY LIFE MAGIC

DATE:

(S) (M) (T) (W) (T) (F) (S)

JOY LEVEL

TODAY'S INTENTIONS

REMINDER TO:

QUOTE FOR TODAY

INSPIRED THOUGHTS:

TODAY'S PRIORITES:

EXERCISE:

TOTAL MINUTES:	
TOTAL STEPS:	

WATER INTAKE:

○ ○ ○ ○ ○ ○ ○

MEAL TRACKER:

BREAKFAST:	LUNCH:
DINNER:	SNACKS:

TO CALL OR EMAIL:

MONEY

MANIFESTED:	GRATEFULLY OUT:

TODAY I AM GRATEFUL FOR:

NOTES:

NEXT DAY GET AHEAD

DAILY LIFE MAGIC

DATE:

(S) (M) (T) (W) (T) (F) (S)

JOY LEVEL

TODAY'S INTENTIONS

REMINDER TO:

QUOTE FOR TODAY

INSPIRED THOUGHTS:

TODAY'S PRIORITES:

EXERCISE:

TOTAL MINUTES:	
TOTAL STEPS:	

WATER INTAKE:

MEAL TRACKER:

BREAKFAST:	LUNCH:
DINNER:	SNACKS:

TO CALL OR EMAIL:

MONEY

MANIFESTED:	GRATEFULLY OUT:

TODAY I AM GRATEFUL FOR:

NOTES:

NEXT DAY GET AHEAD

DAILY LIFE MAGIC

DATE:
S M T W T F S

JOY LEVEL

TODAY'S INTENTIONS

REMINDER TO:

QUOTE FOR TODAY

INSPIRED THOUGHTS :

TODAY'S PRIORITES:

EXERCISE:

TOTAL MINUTES:	
TOTAL STEPS:	

WATER INTAKE:

MEAL TRACKER:

BREAKFAST:	LUNCH:
DINNER:	SNACKS:

TO CALL OR EMAIL:

MONEY

MANIFESTED:	GRATEFULLY OUT:

TODAY I AM GRATEFUL FOR:

NOTES:

NEXT DAY GET AHEAD

DAILY LIFE MAGIC

DATE:

(S) (M) (T) (W) (T) (F) (S)

JOY LEVEL

TODAY'S INTENTIONS

REMINDER TO:

QUOTE FOR TODAY

TODAY'S PRIORITES:

INSPIRED THOUGHTS:

EXERCISE:

TOTAL MINUTES:	
TOTAL STEPS:	

WATER INTAKE:

MEAL TRACKER:

BREAKFAST:	LUNCH:
DINNER:	SNACKS:

TO CALL OR EMAIL:

MONEY

MANIFESTED:	GRATEFULLY OUT:

TODAY I AM GRATEFUL FOR:

NOTES:

NEXT DAY GET AHEAD

DAILY LIFE MAGIC

DATE:
(S) (M) (T) (W) (T) (F) (S)

JOY LEVEL

TODAY'S INTENTIONS

REMINDER TO:

QUOTE FOR TODAY

INSPIRED THOUGHTS :

TODAY'S PRIORITES:

EXERCISE:

TOTAL MINUTES:	
TOTAL STEPS:	

WATER INTAKE:

MEAL TRACKER:

BREAKFAST:	LUNCH:
DINNER:	SNACKS:

TO CALL OR EMAIL:

MONEY

MANIFESTED:	GRATEFULLY OUT:

TODAY I AM GRATEFUL FOR:

NOTES:

NEXT DAY GET AHEAD

DAILY LIFE MAGIC

DATE:
(S) (M) (T) (W) (T) (F) (S)

JOY LEVEL

TODAY'S INTENTIONS

REMINDER TO:

QUOTE FOR TODAY

INSPIRED THOUGHTS：

TODAY'S PRIORITES:

EXERCISE:

TOTAL MINUTES:	
TOTAL STEPS:	

WATER INTAKE:

MEAL TRACKER:

BREAKFAST:	LUNCH:
DINNER:	SNACKS:

TO CALL OR EMAIL:

MONEY

MANIFESTED:	GRATEFULLY OUT:

TODAY I AM GRATEFUL FOR:

NOTES:

NEXT DAY GET AHEAD

DAILY LIFE MAGIC

DATE:

JOY LEVEL

TODAY'S INTENTIONS

REMINDER TO:

QUOTE FOR TODAY

INSPIRED THOUGHTS:

TODAY'S PRIORITES:

EXERCISE:

TOTAL MINUTES:	
TOTAL STEPS:	

WATER INTAKE:

MEAL TRACKER:

BREAKFAST:	LUNCH:
DINNER:	SNACKS:

TO CALL OR EMAIL:

MONEY

MANIFESTED:	GRATEFULLY OUT:

TODAY I AM GRATEFUL FOR:

NOTES:

NEXT DAY GET AHEAD

DAILY LIFE MAGIC

DATE:

(S)(M)(T)(W)(T)(F)(S)

JOY LEVEL

TODAY'S INTENTIONS

REMINDER TO:

QUOTE FOR TODAY

INSPIRED THOUGHTS :

TODAY'S PRIORITES:

EXERCISE:

TOTAL MINUTES:	
TOTAL STEPS:	

WATER INTAKE:

MEAL TRACKER:

TO CALL OR EMAIL:

MONEY

BREAKFAST:	LUNCH:
DINNER:	SNACKS:

MANIFESTED:	GRATEFULLY OUT:

TODAY I AM GRATEFUL FOR:

NOTES:

NEXT DAY GET AHEAD

DAILY LIFE MAGIC

DATE:

Ⓢ Ⓜ Ⓣ Ⓦ Ⓣ Ⓕ Ⓢ

JOY LEVEL

TODAY'S INTENTIONS

REMINDER TO:

QUOTE FOR TODAY

INSPIRED THOUGHTS :

TODAY'S PRIORITES:

EXERCISE:

TOTAL MINUTES:	
TOTAL STEPS:	

WATER INTAKE:

◊ ◊ ◊ ◊ ◊ ◊ ◊ ◊

MEAL TRACKER:

BREAKFAST:	LUNCH:
DINNER:	SNACKS:

TO CALL OR EMAIL:

MONEY

MANIFESTED:	GRATEFULLY OUT:

TODAY I AM GRATEFUL FOR:

NOTES:

NEXT DAY GET AHEAD

DAILY LIFE MAGIC

DATE:
Ⓢ Ⓜ Ⓣ Ⓦ Ⓣ Ⓕ Ⓢ

JOY LEVEL

TODAY'S INTENTIONS

REMINDER TO:

QUOTE FOR TODAY

INSPIRED THOUGHTS:

TODAY'S PRIORITES:

EXERCISE:

TOTAL MINUTES:	
TOTAL STEPS:	

WATER INTAKE:

MEAL TRACKER:

BREAKFAST:	LUNCH:
DINNER:	SNACKS:

TO CALL OR EMAIL:

MONEY

MANIFESTED:	GRATEFULLY OUT:

TODAY I AM GRATEFUL FOR:

NOTES:

NEXT DAY GET AHEAD

DAILY LIFE MAGIC

DATE:

Ⓢ Ⓜ Ⓣ Ⓦ Ⓣ Ⓕ Ⓢ

JOY LEVEL

TODAY'S INTENTIONS

REMINDER TO:

QUOTE FOR TODAY

INSPIRED THOUGHTS :

TODAY'S PRIORITES:

EXERCISE:

TOTAL MINUTES:	
TOTAL STEPS:	

WATER INTAKE:

◯ ◯ ◯ ◯ ◯ ◯ ◯

MEAL TRACKER:

TO CALL OR EMAIL:

MONEY

BREAKFAST:	LUNCH:
DINNER:	SNACKS:

MANIFESTED:	GRATEFULLY OUT:

TODAY I AM GRATEFUL FOR:

NOTES:

NEXT DAY GET AHEAD

DAILY LIFE MAGIC

DATE:
(S) (M) (T) (W) (T) (F) (S)

JOY LEVEL

TODAY'S INTENTIONS

REMINDER TO:

QUOTE FOR TODAY

TODAY'S PRIORITES:

INSPIRED THOUGHTS:

EXERCISE:

TOTAL MINUTES:	
TOTAL STEPS:	

WATER INTAKE:

MEAL TRACKER:

BREAKFAST:	LUNCH:
DINNER:	SNACKS:

TO CALL OR EMAIL:

MONEY

MANIFESTED:	GRATEFULLY OUT:

TODAY I AM GRATEFUL FOR:

NOTES:

NEXT DAY GET AHEAD

DAILY LIFE MAGIC

DATE:

JOY LEVEL

TODAY'S INTENTIONS

REMINDER TO:

QUOTE FOR TODAY

TODAY'S PRIORITES:

INSPIRED THOUGHTS :

EXERCISE:

TOTAL MINUTES:	
TOTAL STEPS:	

WATER INTAKE:

◊ ◊ ◊ ◊ ◊ ◊ ◊

MEAL TRACKER:

BREAKFAST:	LUNCH:
DINNER:	SNACKS:

TO CALL OR EMAIL:

MONEY

MANIFESTED:	GRATEFULLY OUT:

TODAY I AM GRATEFUL FOR:

NOTES:

NEXT DAY GET AHEAD

DAILY LIFE MAGIC

DATE:

(S) (M) (T) (W) (T) (F) (S)

JOY LEVEL

TODAY'S INTENTIONS

REMINDER TO:

QUOTE FOR TODAY

TODAY'S PRIORITES:

INSPIRED THOUGHTS :

EXERCISE:

TOTAL MINUTES:	
TOTAL STEPS:	

WATER INTAKE:

MEAL TRACKER:

BREAKFAST:	LUNCH:
DINNER:	SNACKS:

TO CALL OR EMAIL:

MONEY

MANIFESTED:	GRATEFULLY OUT:

TODAY I AM GRATEFUL FOR:

NOTES:

NEXT DAY GET AHEAD

DAILY LIFE MAGIC

DATE:
S M T W T F S

JOY LEVEL

TODAY'S INTENTIONS

REMINDER TO:

QUOTE FOR TODAY

INSPIRED THOUGHTS :

TODAY'S PRIORITES:

EXERCISE:

TOTAL MINUTES:	
TOTAL STEPS:	

WATER INTAKE:

MEAL TRACKER:

BREAKFAST:	LUNCH:
DINNER:	SNACKS:

TO CALL OR EMAIL:

MONEY

MANIFESTED:	GRATEFULLY OUT:

TODAY I AM GRATEFUL FOR:

NOTES:

NEXT DAY GET AHEAD

DAILY LIFE MAGIC

DATE:
(S) (M) (T) (W) (T) (F) (S)

JOY LEVEL

TODAY'S INTENTIONS

REMINDER TO:

QUOTE FOR TODAY

INSPIRED THOUGHTS :

TODAY'S PRIORITES:

EXERCISE:

TOTAL MINUTES:	
TOTAL STEPS:	

WATER INTAKE:

MEAL TRACKER:

BREAKFAST:	LUNCH:
DINNER:	SNACKS:

TO CALL OR EMAIL:

MONEY

MANIFESTED:	GRATEFULLY OUT:

TODAY I AM GRATEFUL FOR:

NOTES:

NEXT DAY GET AHEAD

DAILY LIFE MAGIC

DATE:

Ⓢ Ⓜ Ⓣ Ⓦ Ⓣ Ⓕ Ⓢ

JOY LEVEL

TODAY'S INTENTIONS

REMINDER TO:

QUOTE FOR TODAY

INSPIRED THOUGHTS:

TODAY'S PRIORITES:

EXERCISE:

TOTAL MINUTES:	
TOTAL STEPS:	

WATER INTAKE:

○ ○ ○ ○ ○ ○ ○

MEAL TRACKER:

BREAKFAST:	LUNCH:
DINNER:	SNACKS:

TO CALL OR EMAIL:

MONEY

MANIFESTED:	GRATEFULLY OUT:

TODAY I AM GRATEFUL FOR:

NOTES:

NEXT DAY GET AHEAD

DAILY LIFE MAGIC

DATE:

(S) (M) (T) (W) (T) (F) (S)

JOY LEVEL

TODAY'S INTENTIONS

REMINDER TO:

QUOTE FOR TODAY

INSPIRED THOUGHTS:

TODAY'S PRIORITIES:

EXERCISE:

TOTAL MINUTES:	
TOTAL STEPS:	

WATER INTAKE:

◯ ◯ ◯ ◯ ◯ ◯ ◯

MEAL TRACKER:

BREAKFAST:	LUNCH:
DINNER:	SNACKS:

TO CALL OR EMAIL:

MONEY

MANIFESTED:	GRATEFULLY OUT:

TODAY I AM GRATEFUL FOR:

NOTES:

NEXT DAY GET AHEAD

DAILY LIFE MAGIC

DATE:

JOY LEVEL

TODAY'S INTENTIONS

REMINDER TO:

QUOTE FOR TODAY

INSPIRED THOUGHTS:

TODAY'S PRIORITES:

EXERCISE:

TOTAL MINUTES:	
TOTAL STEPS:	

WATER INTAKE:

MEAL TRACKER:

BREAKFAST:	LUNCH:
DINNER:	SNACKS:

TO CALL OR EMAIL:

MONEY

MANIFESTED:	GRATEFULLY OUT:

TODAY I AM GRATEFUL FOR:

NOTES:

NEXT DAY GET AHEAD

DAILY LIFE MAGIC

DATE:

(S)(M)(T)(W)(T)(F)(S)

JOY LEVEL

TODAY'S INTENTIONS

REMINDER TO:

QUOTE FOR TODAY

INSPIRED THOUGHTS :

TODAY'S PRIORITES:

EXERCISE:

TOTAL MINUTES:	
TOTAL STEPS:	

WATER INTAKE:

MEAL TRACKER:

TO CALL OR EMAIL:

MONEY

BREAKFAST:	LUNCH:
DINNER:	SNACKS:

MANIFESTED:	GRATEFULLY OUT:

TODAY I AM GRATEFUL FOR:

NOTES:

NEXT DAY GET AHEAD

DAILY LIFE MAGIC

DATE:

Ⓢ Ⓜ Ⓣ Ⓦ Ⓣ Ⓕ Ⓢ

JOY LEVEL

TODAY'S INTENTIONS

REMINDER TO:

QUOTE FOR TODAY

TODAY'S PRIORITES:

INSPIRED THOUGHTS :

EXERCISE:

TOTAL MINUTES:	
TOTAL STEPS:	

WATER INTAKE:

💧💧💧💧💧💧💧

MEAL TRACKER:

BREAKFAST:	LUNCH:
DINNER:	SNACKS:

TO CALL OR EMAIL:

MONEY

MANIFESTED:	GRATEFULLY OUT:

TODAY I AM GRATEFUL FOR:

NOTES:

NEXT DAY GET AHEAD

DAILY LIFE MAGIC

DATE:

Ⓢ Ⓜ Ⓣ Ⓦ Ⓣ Ⓕ Ⓢ

JOY LEVEL

TODAY'S INTENTIONS

REMINDER TO:

QUOTE FOR TODAY

TODAY'S PRIORITES:

INSPIRED THOUGHTS:

EXERCISE:

TOTAL MINUTES:	
TOTAL STEPS:	

WATER INTAKE:

💧 💧 💧 💧 💧 💧

MEAL TRACKER:

BREAKFAST:	LUNCH:
DINNER:	SNACKS:

TO CALL OR EMAIL:

MONEY

MANIFESTED:	GRATEFULLY OUT:

TODAY I AM GRATEFUL FOR:

NOTES:

NEXT DAY GET AHEAD

DAILY LIFE MAGIC

DATE:

Ⓢ Ⓜ Ⓣ Ⓦ Ⓣ Ⓕ Ⓢ

JOY LEVEL

TODAY'S INTENTIONS

REMINDER TO:

QUOTE FOR TODAY

INSPIRED THOUGHTS:

TODAY'S PRIORITES:

EXERCISE:

TOTAL MINUTES:	
TOTAL STEPS:	

WATER INTAKE:

💧 💧 💧 💧 💧 💧 💧

MEAL TRACKER:

BREAKFAST:	LUNCH:
DINNER:	SNACKS:

TO CALL OR EMAIL:

MONEY

MANIFESTED:	GRATEFULLY OUT:

TODAY I AM GRATEFUL FOR:

NOTES:

NEXT DAY GET AHEAD

DAILY LIFE MAGIC

DATE:
(S) (M) (T) (W) (T) (F) (S)

JOY LEVEL

TODAY'S INTENTIONS

REMINDER TO:

QUOTE FOR TODAY

INSPIRED THOUGHTS:

TODAY'S PRIORITIES:

EXERCISE:

TOTAL MINUTES:	
TOTAL STEPS:	

WATER INTAKE:
◇ ◇ ◇ ◇ ◇ ◇ ◇

MEAL TRACKER:

BREAKFAST:	LUNCH:
DINNER:	SNACKS:

TO CALL OR EMAIL:

MONEY

MANIFESTED:	GRATEFULLY OUT:

TODAY I AM GRATEFUL FOR:

NOTES:

NEXT DAY GET AHEAD

DAILY LIFE MAGIC

DATE:

Ⓢ Ⓜ Ⓣ Ⓦ Ⓣ Ⓕ Ⓢ

JOY LEVEL

TODAY'S INTENTIONS

REMINDER TO:

QUOTE FOR TODAY

INSPIRED THOUGHTS :

TODAY'S PRIORITES:

EXERCISE:

TOTAL MINUTES:	
TOTAL STEPS:	

WATER INTAKE:

𖣂 𖣂 𖣂 𖣂 𖣂 𖣂 𖣂

MEAL TRACKER:

TO CALL OR EMAIL:

MONEY

BREAKFAST:	LUNCH:
DINNER:	SNACKS:

MANIFESTED:	GRATEFULLY OUT:

TODAY I AM GRATEFUL FOR:

NOTES:

NEXT DAY GET AHEAD

DAILY LIFE MAGIC

DATE:

(S) (M) (T) (W) (T) (F) (S)

JOY LEVEL

TODAY'S INTENTIONS

REMINDER TO:

QUOTE FOR TODAY

TODAY'S PRIORITES:

INSPIRED THOUGHTS:

EXERCISE:

TOTAL MINUTES:	
TOTAL STEPS:	

WATER INTAKE:

MEAL TRACKER:

BREAKFAST:	LUNCH:
DINNER:	SNACKS:

TO CALL OR EMAIL:

MONEY

MANIFESTED:	GRATEFULLY OUT:

TODAY I AM GRATEFUL FOR:

NOTES:

NEXT DAY GET AHEAD

DAILY LIFE MAGIC

DATE:

(S) (M) (T) (W) (T) (F) (S)

JOY LEVEL

TODAY'S INTENTIONS

REMINDER TO:

QUOTE FOR TODAY

INSPIRED THOUGHTS:

TODAY'S PRIORITES:

EXERCISE:

TOTAL MINUTES:	
TOTAL STEPS:	

WATER INTAKE:

◊ ◊ ◊ ◊ ◊ ◊ ◊

MEAL TRACKER:

TO CALL OR EMAIL:

MONEY

BREAKFAST:	LUNCH:
DINNER:	SNACKS:

MANIFESTED:	GRATEFULLY OUT:

TODAY I AM GRATEFUL FOR:

NOTES:

NEXT DAY GET AHEAD

DAILY LIFE MAGIC

DATE:
(S) (M) (T) (W) (T) (F) (S)

JOY LEVEL

TODAY'S INTENTIONS

REMINDER TO:

QUOTE FOR TODAY

TODAY'S PRIORITES:

INSPIRED THOUGHTS:

EXERCISE:

TOTAL MINUTES:	
TOTAL STEPS:	

WATER INTAKE:

MEAL TRACKER:

BREAKFAST:	LUNCH:
DINNER:	SNACKS:

TO CALL OR EMAIL:

MONEY

MANIFESTED:	GRATEFULLY OUT:

TODAY I AM GRATEFUL FOR:

NOTES:

NEXT DAY GET AHEAD

DAILY LIFE MAGIC

DATE:
Ⓢ Ⓜ Ⓣ Ⓦ Ⓣ Ⓕ Ⓢ

JOY LEVEL

TODAY'S INTENTIONS

REMINDER TO:

QUOTE FOR TODAY

INSPIRED THOUGHTS :

TODAY'S PRIORITES:

EXERCISE:

TOTAL MINUTES:	
TOTAL STEPS:	

WATER INTAKE:
💧💧💧💧💧💧💧

MEAL TRACKER:

BREAKFAST:	LUNCH:
DINNER:	SNACKS:

TO CALL OR EMAIL:

MONEY

MANIFESTED:	GRATEFULLY OUT:

TODAY I AM GRATEFUL FOR:

NOTES:

NEXT DAY GET AHEAD

DAILY LIFE MAGIC

DATE:

S M T W T F S

JOY LEVEL

TODAY'S INTENTIONS

REMINDER TO:

QUOTE FOR TODAY

INSPIRED THOUGHTS :

TODAY'S PRIORITES:

EXERCISE:

TOTAL MINUTES:	
TOTAL STEPS:	

WATER INTAKE:

MEAL TRACKER:

BREAKFAST:	LUNCH:
DINNER:	SNACKS:

TO CALL OR EMAIL:

MONEY

MANIFESTED:	GRATEFULLY OUT:

TODAY I AM GRATEFUL FOR:

NOTES:

NEXT DAY GET AHEAD

DAILY LIFE MAGIC

DATE:
S M T W T F S

JOY LEVEL

TODAY'S INTENTIONS

REMINDER TO:

QUOTE FOR TODAY

INSPIRED THOUGHTS:

TODAY'S PRIORITES:

EXERCISE:

TOTAL MINUTES:	
TOTAL STEPS:	

WATER INTAKE:

MEAL TRACKER:

BREAKFAST:	LUNCH:
DINNER:	SNACKS:

TO CALL OR EMAIL:

MONEY

MANIFESTED:	GRATEFULLY OUT:

TODAY I AM GRATEFUL FOR:

NOTES:

NEXT DAY GET AHEAD

DAILY LIFE MAGIC

DATE:
(S) (M) (T) (W) (T) (F) (S)

JOY LEVEL

TODAY'S INTENTIONS

REMINDER TO:

QUOTE FOR TODAY

INSPIRED THOUGHTS:

TODAY'S PRIORITES:

EXERCISE:

TOTAL MINUTES:	
TOTAL STEPS:	

WATER INTAKE:

◊ ◊ ◊ ◊ ◊ ◊ ◊

MEAL TRACKER:

BREAKFAST:	LUNCH:
DINNER:	SNACKS:

TO CALL OR EMAIL:

MONEY

MANIFESTED:	GRATEFULLY OUT:

TODAY I AM GRATEFUL FOR:

NOTES:

NEXT DAY GET AHEAD

DAILY LIFE MAGIC

DATE:
(S) (M) (T) (W) (T) (F) (S)

JOY LEVEL

TODAY'S INTENTIONS

REMINDER TO:

QUOTE FOR TODAY

INSPIRED THOUGHTS:

TODAY'S PRIORITIES:

EXERCISE:

TOTAL MINUTES:	
TOTAL STEPS:	

WATER INTAKE:

MEAL TRACKER:

BREAKFAST:	LUNCH:
DINNER:	SNACKS:

TO CALL OR EMAIL:

MONEY

MANIFESTED:	GRATEFULLY OUT:

TODAY I AM GRATEFUL FOR:

NOTES:

NEXT DAY GET AHEAD

DAILY LIFE MAGIC

DATE:
Ⓢ Ⓜ Ⓣ Ⓦ Ⓣ Ⓕ Ⓢ

JOY LEVEL

😄 🙂 😐 🙁 😢

QUOTE FOR TODAY

TODAY'S INTENTIONS

REMINDER TO:

INSPIRED THOUGHTS:

TODAY'S PRIORITES:

EXERCISE:

TOTAL MINUTES:	
TOTAL STEPS:	

WATER INTAKE:

💧💧💧💧💧💧💧

MEAL TRACKER:

BREAKFAST:	LUNCH:
DINNER:	SNACKS:

TO CALL OR EMAIL:

MONEY

MANIFESTED:	GRATEFULLY OUT:

TODAY I AM GRATEFUL FOR:

NOTES:

NEXT DAY GET AHEAD

DAILY LIFE MAGIC

DATE:
(S) (M) (T) (W) (T) (F) (S)

JOY LEVEL

TODAY'S INTENTIONS

REMINDER TO:

QUOTE FOR TODAY

INSPIRED THOUGHTS :

TODAY'S PRIORITES:

EXERCISE:

TOTAL MINUTES:	
TOTAL STEPS:	

WATER INTAKE:
○ ○ ○ ○ ○ ○ ○

MEAL TRACKER:

BREAKFAST:	LUNCH:
DINNER:	SNACKS:

TO CALL OR EMAIL:

MONEY

MANIFESTED:	GRATEFULLY OUT:

TODAY I AM GRATEFUL FOR:

NOTES:

NEXT DAY GET AHEAD

DAILY LIFE MAGIC

DATE:

    S M T W T F S

JOY LEVEL

TODAY'S INTENTIONS

REMINDER TO:

QUOTE FOR TODAY

INSPIRED THOUGHTS :

TODAY'S PRIORITES:

EXERCISE:

TOTAL MINUTES:	
TOTAL STEPS:	

WATER INTAKE:

○ ○ ○ ○ ○ ○ ○

MEAL TRACKER:

BREAKFAST:	LUNCH:
DINNER:	SNACKS:

TO CALL OR EMAIL:

MONEY

MANIFESTED:	GRATEFULLY OUT:

TODAY I AM GRATEFUL FOR:

NOTES:

NEXT DAY GET AHEAD

DAILY LIFE MAGIC

DATE:

(S) (M) (T) (W) (T) (F) (S)

JOY LEVEL

TODAY'S INTENTIONS

REMINDER TO:

QUOTE FOR TODAY

INSPIRED THOUGHTS:

TODAY'S PRIORITES:

EXERCISE:

TOTAL MINUTES:	
TOTAL STEPS:	

WATER INTAKE:

MEAL TRACKER:

BREAKFAST:	LUNCH:
DINNER:	SNACKS:

TO CALL OR EMAIL:

MONEY

MANIFESTED:	GRATEFULLY OUT:

TODAY I AM GRATEFUL FOR:

NOTES:

NEXT DAY GET AHEAD

DAILY LIFE MAGIC

DATE:

JOY LEVEL

TODAY'S INTENTIONS

REMINDER TO:

QUOTE FOR TODAY

INSPIRED THOUGHTS:

TODAY'S PRIORITES:

EXERCISE:

TOTAL MINUTES:	
TOTAL STEPS:	

WATER INTAKE:

○ ○ ○ ○ ○ ○

MEAL TRACKER:

BREAKFAST:	LUNCH:
DINNER:	SNACKS:

TO CALL OR EMAIL:

MONEY

MANIFESTED:	GRATEFULLY OUT:

TODAY I AM GRATEFUL FOR:

NOTES:

NEXT DAY GET AHEAD

DAILY LIFE MAGIC

DATE:
(S) (M) (T) (W) (T) (F) (S)

JOY LEVEL

TODAY'S INTENTIONS

REMINDER TO:

QUOTE FOR TODAY

TODAY'S PRIORITIES:

INSPIRED THOUGHTS:

EXERCISE:

TOTAL MINUTES:	
TOTAL STEPS:	

WATER INTAKE:

MEAL TRACKER:

BREAKFAST:	LUNCH:
DINNER:	SNACKS:

TO CALL OR EMAIL:

MONEY

MANIFESTED:	GRATEFULLY OUT:

TODAY I AM GRATEFUL FOR:

NOTES:

NEXT DAY GET AHEAD

DAILY LIFE MAGIC

DATE:
Ⓢ Ⓜ Ⓣ Ⓦ Ⓣ Ⓕ Ⓢ

JOY LEVEL

TODAY'S INTENTIONS

REMINDER TO:

QUOTE FOR TODAY

INSPIRED THOUGHTS:

TODAY'S PRIORITES:

EXERCISE:

TOTAL MINUTES:	
TOTAL STEPS:	

WATER INTAKE:
💧💧💧💧💧💧💧

MEAL TRACKER:

TO CALL OR EMAIL:

MONEY

BREAKFAST:	LUNCH:
DINNER:	SNACKS:

MANIFESTED:	GRATEFULLY OUT:

TODAY I AM GRATEFUL FOR:

NOTES:

NEXT DAY GET AHEAD

DAILY LIFE MAGIC

DATE:
(S) (M) (T) (W) (T) (F) (S)

JOY LEVEL

TODAY'S INTENTIONS

REMINDER TO:

QUOTE FOR TODAY

INSPIRED THOUGHTS :

TODAY'S PRIORITES:

EXERCISE:

TOTAL MINUTES:	
TOTAL STEPS:	

WATER INTAKE:

MEAL TRACKER:

BREAKFAST:	LUNCH:
DINNER:	SNACKS:

TO CALL OR EMAIL:

MONEY

MANIFESTED:	GRATEFULLY OUT:

TODAY I AM GRATEFUL FOR:

NOTES:

NEXT DAY GET AHEAD

DAILY LIFE MAGIC

DATE:
(S) (M) (T) (W) (T) (F) (S)

JOY LEVEL

TODAY'S INTENTIONS

REMINDER TO:

QUOTE FOR TODAY

INSPIRED THOUGHTS :

TODAY'S PRIORITES:

EXERCISE:

TOTAL MINUTES:	
TOTAL STEPS:	

WATER INTAKE:

MEAL TRACKER:

BREAKFAST:	LUNCH:
DINNER:	SNACKS:

TO CALL OR EMAIL:

MONEY

MANIFESTED:	GRATEFULLY OUT:

TODAY I AM GRATEFUL FOR:

NOTES:

NEXT DAY GET AHEAD

DAILY LIFE MAGIC

DATE:

(S) (M) (T) (W) (T) (F) (S)

JOY LEVEL

😊 😃 😐 ☹️ 😢

TODAY'S INTENTIONS

REMINDER TO:

QUOTE FOR TODAY

INSPIRED THOUGHTS:

TODAY'S PRIORITIES:

EXERCISE:

TOTAL MINUTES:	
TOTAL STEPS:	

WATER INTAKE:

○ ○ ○ ○ ○ ○ ○ ○

MEAL TRACKER:

BREAKFAST:	LUNCH:
DINNER:	SNACKS:

TO CALL OR EMAIL:

MONEY

MANIFESTED:	GRATEFULLY OUT:

TODAY I AM GRATEFUL FOR:

NOTES:

NEXT DAY GET AHEAD

DAILY LIFE MAGIC

DATE:

JOY LEVEL

TODAY'S INTENTIONS

REMINDER TO:

QUOTE FOR TODAY

INSPIRED THOUGHTS :

TODAY'S PRIORITES:

EXERCISE:

TOTAL MINUTES:	
TOTAL STEPS:	

WATER INTAKE:

MEAL TRACKER:

BREAKFAST:	LUNCH:
DINNER:	SNACKS:

TO CALL OR EMAIL:

MONEY

MANIFESTED:	GRATEFULLY OUT:

TODAY I AM GRATEFUL FOR:

NOTES:

NEXT DAY GET AHEAD

DAILY LIFE MAGIC

DATE:

(S) (M) (T) (W) (T) (F) (S)

JOY LEVEL

TODAY'S INTENTIONS

REMINDER TO:

QUOTE FOR TODAY

INSPIRED THOUGHTS :

TODAY'S PRIORITES:

EXERCISE:

TOTAL MINUTES:	
TOTAL STEPS:	

WATER INTAKE:

MEAL TRACKER:

BREAKFAST:	LUNCH:
DINNER:	SNACKS:

TO CALL OR EMAIL:

MONEY

MANIFESTED:	GRATEFULLY OUT:

TODAY I AM GRATEFUL FOR:

NOTES:

NEXT DAY GET AHEAD

DAILY LIFE MAGIC

DATE:

Ⓢ Ⓜ Ⓣ Ⓦ Ⓣ Ⓕ Ⓢ

JOY LEVEL

TODAY'S INTENTIONS

REMINDER TO:

QUOTE FOR TODAY

TODAY'S PRIORITES:

INSPIRED THOUGHTS :

EXERCISE:

TOTAL MINUTES:	
TOTAL STEPS:	

WATER INTAKE:
💧💧💧💧💧💧💧

MEAL TRACKER:

BREAKFAST:	LUNCH:
DINNER:	SNACKS:

TO CALL OR EMAIL:

MONEY

MANIFESTED:	GRATEFULLY OUT:

TODAY I AM GRATEFUL FOR:

NOTES:

NEXT DAY GET AHEAD

DAILY LIFE MAGIC

DATE:
(S) (M) (T) (W) (T) (F) (S)

JOY LEVEL

TODAY'S INTENTIONS

REMINDER TO:

QUOTE FOR TODAY

INSPIRED THOUGHTS:

TODAY'S PRIORITES:

EXERCISE:

TOTAL MINUTES:	
TOTAL STEPS:	

WATER INTAKE:

MEAL TRACKER:

BREAKFAST:	LUNCH:
DINNER:	SNACKS:

TO CALL OR EMAIL:

MONEY

MANIFESTED:	GRATEFULLY OUT:

TODAY I AM GRATEFUL FOR:

NOTES:

NEXT DAY GET AHEAD

DAILY LIFE MAGIC

DATE:

JOY LEVEL

TODAY'S INTENTIONS

REMINDER TO:

QUOTE FOR TODAY

INSPIRED THOUGHTS :

TODAY'S PRIORITES:

EXERCISE:

TOTAL MINUTES:	
TOTAL STEPS:	

WATER INTAKE:

MEAL TRACKER:

BREAKFAST:	LUNCH:
DINNER:	SNACKS:

TO CALL OR EMAIL:

MONEY

MANIFESTED:	GRATEFULLY OUT:

TODAY I AM GRATEFUL FOR:

NOTES:

NEXT DAY GET AHEAD

DAILY LIFE MAGIC

DATE:
(S) (M) (T) (W) (T) (F) (S)

JOY LEVEL

TODAY'S INTENTIONS

REMINDER TO:

QUOTE FOR TODAY

TODAY'S PRIORITIES:

INSPIRED THOUGHTS :

EXERCISE:

TOTAL MINUTES:	
TOTAL STEPS:	

WATER INTAKE:

MEAL TRACKER:

BREAKFAST:	LUNCH:
DINNER:	SNACKS:

TO CALL OR EMAIL:

MONEY

MANIFESTED:	GRATEFULLY OUT:

TODAY I AM GRATEFUL FOR:

NOTES:

NEXT DAY GET AHEAD

DAILY LIFE MAGIC

DATE:

JOY LEVEL

TODAY'S INTENTIONS

REMINDER TO:

QUOTE FOR TODAY

INSPIRED THOUGHTS :

TODAY'S PRIORITES:

EXERCISE:

TOTAL MINUTES:	
TOTAL STEPS:	

WATER INTAKE:

MEAL TRACKER:

BREAKFAST:	LUNCH:
DINNER:	SNACKS:

TO CALL OR EMAIL:

MONEY

MANIFESTED:	GRATEFULLY OUT:

TODAY I AM GRATEFUL FOR:

NOTES:

NEXT DAY GET AHEAD

DAILY LIFE MAGIC

DATE:

(S) (M) (T) (W) (T) (F) (S)

JOY LEVEL

😄 🙂 😐 🙁 😢

TODAY'S INTENTIONS

REMINDER TO:

QUOTE FOR TODAY

INSPIRED THOUGHTS:

TODAY'S PRIORITES:

EXERCISE:

TOTAL MINUTES:	
TOTAL STEPS:	

WATER INTAKE:

💧 💧 💧 💧 💧 💧 💧

MEAL TRACKER:

BREAKFAST:	LUNCH:
DINNER:	SNACKS:

TO CALL OR EMAIL:

MONEY

MANIFESTED:	GRATEFULLY OUT:

TODAY I AM GRATEFUL FOR:

NOTES:

NEXT DAY GET AHEAD

DAILY LIFE MAGIC

DATE:
Ⓢ Ⓜ Ⓣ Ⓦ Ⓣ Ⓕ Ⓢ

JOY LEVEL

TODAY'S INTENTIONS

REMINDER TO:

QUOTE FOR TODAY

INSPIRED THOUGHTS:

TODAY'S PRIORITIES:

EXERCISE:

TOTAL MINUTES:	
TOTAL STEPS:	

WATER INTAKE:
💧💧💧💧💧💧💧

MEAL TRACKER:

TO CALL OR EMAIL:

MONEY

BREAKFAST:	LUNCH:
DINNER:	SNACKS:

MANIFESTED:	GRATEFULLY OUT:

TODAY I AM GRATEFUL FOR:

NOTES:

NEXT DAY GET AHEAD

DAILY LIFE MAGIC

DATE:
Ⓢ Ⓜ Ⓣ Ⓦ Ⓣ Ⓕ Ⓢ

JOY LEVEL

TODAY'S INTENTIONS

REMINDER TO:

QUOTE FOR TODAY

INSPIRED THOUGHTS:

TODAY'S PRIORITES:

EXERCISE:

TOTAL MINUTES:	
TOTAL STEPS:	

WATER INTAKE:

MEAL TRACKER:

BREAKFAST:	LUNCH:
DINNER:	SNACKS:

TO CALL OR EMAIL:

MONEY

MANIFESTED:	GRATEFULLY OUT:

TODAY I AM GRATEFUL FOR:

NOTES:

NEXT DAY GET AHEAD

DAILY LIFE MAGIC

DATE:

JOY LEVEL

TODAY'S INTENTIONS

REMINDER TO:

QUOTE FOR TODAY

INSPIRED THOUGHTS :

TODAY'S PRIORITES:

EXERCISE:

TOTAL MINUTES:	
TOTAL STEPS:	

WATER INTAKE:

MEAL TRACKER:

BREAKFAST:	LUNCH:
DINNER:	SNACKS:

TO CALL OR EMAIL:

MONEY

MANIFESTED:	GRATEFULLY OUT:

TODAY I AM GRATEFUL FOR:

NOTES:

NEXT DAY GET AHEAD

DAILY LIFE MAGIC

DATE:
(S) (M) (T) (W) (T) (F) (S)

JOY LEVEL

TODAY'S INTENTIONS

REMINDER TO:

QUOTE FOR TODAY

INSPIRED THOUGHTS :

TODAY'S PRIORITES:

EXERCISE:

TOTAL MINUTES:	
TOTAL STEPS:	

WATER INTAKE:
◯ ◯ ◯ ◯ ◯ ◯

MEAL TRACKER:

BREAKFAST:	LUNCH:
DINNER:	SNACKS:

TO CALL OR EMAIL:

MONEY

MANIFESTED:	GRATEFULLY OUT:

TODAY I AM GRATEFUL FOR:

NOTES:

NEXT DAY GET AHEAD

DAILY LIFE MAGIC

DATE:
(S) (M) (T) (W) (T) (F) (S)

JOY LEVEL

TODAY'S INTENTIONS

REMINDER TO:

QUOTE FOR TODAY

INSPIRED THOUGHTS :

TODAY'S PRIORITES:

EXERCISE:

TOTAL MINUTES:	
TOTAL STEPS:	

WATER INTAKE:

MEAL TRACKER:

BREAKFAST:	LUNCH:
DINNER:	SNACKS:

TO CALL OR EMAIL:

MONEY

MANIFESTED:	GRATEFULLY OUT:

TODAY I AM GRATEFUL FOR:

NOTES:

NEXT DAY GET AHEAD

DAILY LIFE MAGIC

DATE:

(S) (M) (T) (W) (T) (F) (S)

JOY LEVEL

😄 🙂 😐 🙁 😢

QUOTE FOR TODAY

TODAY'S INTENTIONS

REMINDER TO:

INSPIRED THOUGHTS:

_____
_____
_____
_____
_____
_____
_____
_____
_____
_____
_____

TODAY'S PRIORITES:

_____
_____
_____
_____
_____
_____
_____
_____
_____
_____
_____

EXERCISE:

TOTAL MINUTES:	
TOTAL STEPS:	

WATER INTAKE:

💧💧💧💧💧💧

MEAL TRACKER:

BREAKFAST:	LUNCH:
DINNER:	SNACKS:

TO CALL OR EMAIL:

_____
_____
_____
_____
_____

MONEY

MANIFESTED:	GRATEFULLY OUT:

TODAY I AM GRATEFUL FOR:

_____
_____
_____
_____
_____
_____

NOTES:

_____
_____
_____
_____
_____
_____
_____

NEXT DAY GET AHEAD

_____
_____
_____
_____
_____
_____

DAILY LIFE MAGIC

DATE:

(S) (M) (T) (W) (T) (F) (S)

JOY LEVEL

TODAY'S INTENTIONS

REMINDER TO:

QUOTE FOR TODAY

TODAY'S PRIORITES:

INSPIRED THOUGHTS:

EXERCISE:

TOTAL MINUTES:	
TOTAL STEPS:	

WATER INTAKE:

MEAL TRACKER:

BREAKFAST:	LUNCH:
DINNER:	SNACKS:

TO CALL OR EMAIL:

MONEY

MANIFESTED:	GRATEFULLY OUT:

TODAY I AM GRATEFUL FOR:

NOTES:

NEXT DAY GET AHEAD

DAILY LIFE MAGIC

DATE:
(S) (M) (T) (W) (T) (F) (S)

JOY LEVEL

TODAY'S INTENTIONS

REMINDER TO:

QUOTE FOR TODAY

INSPIRED THOUGHTS：

TODAY'S PRIORITES:

EXERCISE:

TOTAL MINUTES:	
TOTAL STEPS:	

WATER INTAKE:

○ ○ ○ ○ ○ ○ ○

MEAL TRACKER:

BREAKFAST:	LUNCH:
DINNER:	SNACKS:

TO CALL OR EMAIL:

MONEY

MANIFESTED:	GRATEFULLY OUT:

TODAY I AM GRATEFUL FOR:

NOTES:

NEXT DAY GET AHEAD

DAILY LIFE MAGIC

DATE:

(S) (M) (T) (W) (T) (F) (S)

JOY LEVEL

TODAY'S INTENTIONS

REMINDER TO:

QUOTE FOR TODAY

INSPIRED THOUGHTS:

TODAY'S PRIORITES:

EXERCISE:

TOTAL MINUTES:	
TOTAL STEPS:	

WATER INTAKE:

MEAL TRACKER:

BREAKFAST:	LUNCH:
DINNER:	SNACKS:

TO CALL OR EMAIL:

MONEY

MANIFESTED:	GRATEFULLY OUT:

TODAY I AM GRATEFUL FOR:

NOTES:

NEXT DAY GET AHEAD

DAILY LIFE MAGIC

DATE:
(S) (M) (T) (W) (T) (F) (S)

JOY LEVEL

QUOTE FOR TODAY

TODAY'S INTENTIONS

REMINDER TO:

INSPIRED THOUGHTS:

TODAY'S PRIORITES:

EXERCISE:

TOTAL MINUTES:	
TOTAL STEPS:	

WATER INTAKE:

MEAL TRACKER:

BREAKFAST:	LUNCH:
DINNER:	SNACKS:

TO CALL OR EMAIL:

MONEY

MANIFESTED:	GRATEFULLY OUT:

TODAY I AM GRATEFUL FOR:

NOTES:

NEXT DAY GET AHEAD

DAILY LIFE MAGIC

DATE:

JOY LEVEL

TODAY'S INTENTIONS

REMINDER TO:

QUOTE FOR TODAY

INSPIRED THOUGHTS :

TODAY'S PRIORITES:

EXERCISE:

TOTAL MINUTES:	
TOTAL STEPS:	

WATER INTAKE:

○ ○ ○ ○ ○ ○ ○

MEAL TRACKER:

TO CALL OR EMAIL:

MONEY

BREAKFAST:	LUNCH:
DINNER:	SNACKS:

MANIFESTED:	GRATEFULLY OUT:

TODAY I AM GRATEFUL FOR:

NOTES:

NEXT DAY GET AHEAD

DAILY LIFE MAGIC

DATE:

(S)(M)(T)(W)(T)(F)(S)

JOY LEVEL

😄 🙂 😐 🙁 😢

QUOTE FOR TODAY

TODAY'S INTENTIONS

REMINDER TO:

INSPIRED THOUGHTS:

TODAY'S PRIORITES:

EXERCISE:

TOTAL MINUTES:	
TOTAL STEPS:	

WATER INTAKE:

💧💧💧💧💧💧

MEAL TRACKER:

BREAKFAST:	LUNCH:
DINNER:	SNACKS:

TO CALL OR EMAIL:

MONEY

MANIFESTED:	GRATEFULLY OUT:

TODAY I AM GRATEFUL FOR:

NOTES:

NEXT DAY GET AHEAD

DAILY LIFE MAGIC

DATE:

Ⓢ Ⓜ Ⓣ Ⓦ Ⓣ Ⓕ Ⓢ

JOY LEVEL

TODAY'S INTENTIONS

REMINDER TO:

QUOTE FOR TODAY

INSPIRED THOUGHTS:

TODAY'S PRIORITES:

EXERCISE:

TOTAL MINUTES:	
TOTAL STEPS:	

WATER INTAKE:

💧💧💧💧💧💧💧

MEAL TRACKER:

BREAKFAST:	LUNCH:
DINNER:	SNACKS:

TO CALL OR EMAIL:

MONEY

MANIFESTED:	GRATEFULLY OUT:

TODAY I AM GRATEFUL FOR:

NOTES:

NEXT DAY GET AHEAD

DAILY LIFE MAGIC

DATE:

(S) (M) (T) (W) (T) (F) (S)

JOY LEVEL

TODAY'S INTENTIONS

REMINDER TO:

QUOTE FOR TODAY

INSPIRED THOUGHTS:

TODAY'S PRIORITES:

EXERCISE:

TOTAL MINUTES:	
TOTAL STEPS:	

WATER INTAKE:

○ ○ ○ ○ ○ ○ ○

MEAL TRACKER:

BREAKFAST:	LUNCH:
DINNER:	SNACKS:

TO CALL OR EMAIL:

MONEY

MANIFESTED:	GRATEFULLY OUT:

TODAY I AM GRATEFUL FOR:

NOTES:

NEXT DAY GET AHEAD

DAILY LIFE MAGIC

DATE:

JOY LEVEL

TODAY'S INTENTIONS

REMINDER TO:

QUOTE FOR TODAY

INSPIRED THOUGHTS :

TODAY'S PRIORITES:

EXERCISE:

TOTAL MINUTES:	
TOTAL STEPS:	

WATER INTAKE:

○ ○ ○ ○ ○ ○ ○

MEAL TRACKER:

BREAKFAST:	LUNCH:
DINNER:	SNACKS:

TO CALL OR EMAIL:

MONEY

MANIFESTED:	GRATEFULLY OUT:

TODAY I AM GRATEFUL FOR:

NOTES:

NEXT DAY GET AHEAD

DAILY LIFE MAGIC

DATE:
(S) (M) (T) (W) (T) (F) (S)

JOY LEVEL

QUOTE FOR TODAY

TODAY'S INTENTIONS

REMINDER TO:

INSPIRED THOUGHTS :

TODAY'S PRIORITES:

EXERCISE:

TOTAL MINUTES:	
TOTAL STEPS:	

WATER INTAKE:

MEAL TRACKER:

BREAKFAST:	LUNCH:
DINNER:	SNACKS:

TO CALL OR EMAIL:

MONEY

MANIFESTED:	GRATEFULLY OUT:

TODAY I AM GRATEFUL FOR:

NOTES:

NEXT DAY GET AHEAD

DAILY LIFE MAGIC

DATE:

JOY LEVEL

TODAY'S INTENTIONS

REMINDER TO:

QUOTE FOR TODAY

INSPIRED THOUGHTS :

TODAY'S PRIORITES:

EXERCISE:

TOTAL MINUTES:	
TOTAL STEPS:	

WATER INTAKE:

MEAL TRACKER:

TO CALL OR EMAIL:

MONEY

BREAKFAST:	LUNCH:
DINNER:	SNACKS:

MANIFESTED:	GRATEFULLY OUT:

TODAY I AM GRATEFUL FOR:

NOTES:

NEXT DAY GET AHEAD

DAILY LIFE MAGIC

DATE:
(S) (M) (T) (W) (T) (F) (S)

JOY LEVEL

TODAY'S INTENTIONS

REMINDER TO:

QUOTE FOR TODAY

TODAY'S PRIORITIES:

INSPIRED THOUGHTS:

EXERCISE:

TOTAL MINUTES:	
TOTAL STEPS:	

WATER INTAKE:

MEAL TRACKER:

BREAKFAST:	LUNCH:
DINNER:	SNACKS:

TO CALL OR EMAIL:

MONEY

MANIFESTED:	GRATEFULLY OUT:

TODAY I AM GRATEFUL FOR:

NOTES:

NEXT DAY GET AHEAD

DAILY LIFE MAGIC

DATE:

JOY LEVEL

TODAY'S INTENTIONS

REMINDER TO:

QUOTE FOR TODAY

EXERCISE:

TOTAL MINUTES:	
TOTAL STEPS:	

WATER INTAKE:

MEAL TRACKER:

BREAKFAST:	LUNCH:
DINNER:	SNACKS:

TODAY'S PRIORITES:

INSPIRED THOUGHTS :

TO CALL OR EMAIL:

MONEY

MANIFESTED:	GRATEFULLY OUT:

TODAY I AM GRATEFUL FOR:

NOTES:

NEXT DAY GET AHEAD

DAILY LIFE MAGIC

DATE:
(S) (M) (T) (W) (T) (F) (S)

JOY LEVEL

TODAY'S INTENTIONS

REMINDER TO:

QUOTE FOR TODAY

INSPIRED THOUGHTS:

TODAY'S PRIORITIES:

EXERCISE:

TOTAL MINUTES:	
TOTAL STEPS:	

WATER INTAKE:
○ ○ ○ ○ ○ ○ ○

MEAL TRACKER:

BREAKFAST:	LUNCH:
DINNER:	SNACKS:

TO CALL OR EMAIL:

MONEY

MANIFESTED:	GRATEFULLY OUT:

TODAY I AM GRATEFUL FOR:

NOTES:

NEXT DAY GET AHEAD

DAILY LIFE MAGIC

DATE:
(S) (M) (T) (W) (T) (F) (S)

JOY LEVEL

TODAY'S INTENTIONS

REMINDER TO:

QUOTE FOR TODAY

TODAY'S PRIORITES:

INSPIRED THOUGHTS :

EXERCISE:

TOTAL MINUTES:	
TOTAL STEPS:	

WATER INTAKE:

◊ ◊ ◊ ◊ ◊ ◊ ◊

MEAL TRACKER:

BREAKFAST:	LUNCH:
DINNER:	SNACKS:

TO CALL OR EMAIL:

MONEY

MANIFESTED:	GRATEFULLY OUT:

TODAY I AM GRATEFUL FOR:

NOTES:

NEXT DAY GET AHEAD

DAILY LIFE MAGIC

DATE:

(S) (M) (T) (W) (T) (F) (S)

JOY LEVEL

TODAY'S INTENTIONS

REMINDER TO:

QUOTE FOR TODAY

INSPIRED THOUGHTS:

TODAY'S PRIORITES:

EXERCISE:

TOTAL MINUTES:	
TOTAL STEPS:	

WATER INTAKE:

○ ○ ○ ○ ○ ○ ○

MEAL TRACKER:

BREAKFAST:	LUNCH:
DINNER:	SNACKS:

TO CALL OR EMAIL:

MONEY

MANIFESTED:	GRATEFULLY OUT:

TODAY I AM GRATEFUL FOR:

NOTES:

NEXT DAY GET AHEAD

DAILY LIFE MAGIC

DATE:

(S) (M)

JOY LEVEL

😃 🙂 😐 🙁 😢

TODAY'S INTENTIONS

REMINDER TO:

QUOTE FOR TODAY

INSPIRED THOUGHTS :

TODAY'S PRIORITES:

EXERCISE:

TOTAL MINUTES:	
TOTAL STEPS:	

WATER INTAKE:

💧💧💧💧💧💧💧

MEAL TRACKER:

BREAKFAST:	LUNCH:
DINNER:	SNACKS:

TO CALL OR EMAIL:

MONEY

MANIFESTED:	GRATEFULLY OUT:

TODAY I AM GRATEFUL FOR:

NOTES:

NEXT DAY GET AHEAD

DAILY LIFE MAGIC

DATE:
(S) (M) (T) (W) (T) (F) (S)

JOY LEVEL

TODAY'S INTENTIONS

REMINDER TO:

QUOTE FOR TODAY

TODAY'S PRIORITES:

INSPIRED THOUGHTS:

EXERCISE:

TOTAL MINUTES:	
TOTAL STEPS:	

WATER INTAKE:

MEAL TRACKER:

BREAKFAST:	LUNCH:
DINNER:	SNACKS:

TO CALL OR EMAIL:

MONEY

MANIFESTED:	GRATEFULLY OUT:

TODAY I AM GRATEFUL FOR:

NOTES:

NEXT DAY GET AHEAD

DAILY LIFE MAGIC

DATE:

Ⓢ Ⓜ Ⓣ Ⓦ

JOY LEVEL

   😕 😢

TODAY'S INTENTIONS

REMINDER TO:

QUOTE FOR TODAY

INSPIRED THOUGHTS :

TODAY'S PRIORITES:

EXERCISE:

TOTAL MINUTES:	
TOTAL STEPS:	

WATER INTAKE:

💧💧💧💧💧💧💧

MEAL TRACKER:

BREAKFAST:	LUNCH:
DINNER:	SNACKS:

TO CALL OR EMAIL:

MONEY

MANIFESTED:	GRATEFULLY OUT:

TODAY I AM GRATEFUL FOR:

NOTES:

NEXT DAY GET AHEAD

DAILY LIFE MAGIC

DATE:
(S) (M) (T) (W) (T) (F) (S)

JOY LEVEL

TODAY'S INTENTIONS

REMINDER TO:

QUOTE FOR TODAY

TODAY'S PRIORITIES:

INSPIRED THOUGHTS:

EXERCISE:

TOTAL MINUTES:	
TOTAL STEPS:	

WATER INTAKE:

MEAL TRACKER:

BREAKFAST:	LUNCH:
DINNER:	SNACKS:

TO CALL OR EMAIL:

MONEY

MANIFESTED:	GRATEFULLY OUT:

TODAY I AM GRATEFUL FOR:

NOTES:

NEXT DAY GET AHEAD

DAILY LIFE MAGIC

DATE:
Ⓢ Ⓜ Ⓣ Ⓦ Ⓣ Ⓕ Ⓢ

JOY LEVEL

TODAY'S INTENTIONS

REMINDER TO:

QUOTE FOR TODAY

EXERCISE:

TOTAL MINUTES:	
TOTAL STEPS:	

WATER INTAKE:
💧 💧 💧 💧 💧 💧

MEAL TRACKER:

BREAKFAST:	LUNCH:
DINNER:	SNACKS:

TODAY'S PRIORITES:

_____
_____
_____
_____
_____
_____
_____
_____
_____
_____

TO CALL OR EMAIL:

_____
_____
_____
_____
_____

INSPIRED THOUGHTS :

_____
_____
_____
_____
_____
_____
_____
_____
_____
_____

MONEY

MANIFESTED:	GRATEFULLY OUT:

TODAY I AM GRATEFUL FOR:

_____
_____
_____
_____
_____

NOTES:

_____
_____
_____
_____
_____

NEXT DAY GET AHEAD

_____
_____
_____
_____
_____

DAILY LIFE MAGIC

DATE:
(S) (M) (T) (W) (T) (F) (S)

JOY LEVEL

TODAY'S INTENTIONS

REMINDER TO:

QUOTE FOR TODAY

TODAY'S PRIORITIES:

INSPIRED THOUGHTS:

EXERCISE:

TOTAL MINUTES:	
TOTAL STEPS:	

WATER INTAKE:

MEAL TRACKER:

BREAKFAST:	LUNCH:
DINNER:	SNACKS:

TO CALL OR EMAIL:

MONEY

MANIFESTED:	GRATEFULLY OUT:

TODAY I AM GRATEFUL FOR:

NOTES:

NEXT DAY GET AHEAD

DAILY LIFE MAGIC

DATE:
Ⓢ Ⓜ Ⓣ Ⓦ Ⓣ Ⓕ Ⓢ

JOY LEVEL

TODAY'S INTENTIONS

REMINDER TO:

QUOTE FOR TODAY

INSPIRED THOUGHTS :

TODAY'S PRIORITES:

EXERCISE:

TOTAL MINUTES:	
TOTAL STEPS:	

WATER INTAKE:
◊ ◊ ◊ ◊ ◊ ◊ ◊

MEAL TRACKER:

BREAKFAST:	LUNCH:
DINNER:	SNACKS:

TO CALL OR EMAIL:

MONEY

MANIFESTED:	GRATEFULLY OUT:

TODAY I AM GRATEFUL FOR:

NOTES:

NEXT DAY GET AHEAD

DAILY LIFE MAGIC

DATE:
(S) (M) (T) (W) (T) (F) (S)

JOY LEVEL

TODAY'S INTENTIONS

REMINDER TO:

QUOTE FOR TODAY

TODAY'S PRIORITIES:

INSPIRED THOUGHTS:

EXERCISE:

TOTAL MINUTES:	
TOTAL STEPS:	

WATER INTAKE:

MEAL TRACKER:

BREAKFAST:	LUNCH:
DINNER:	SNACKS:

TO CALL OR EMAIL:

MONEY

MANIFESTED:	GRATEFULLY OUT:

TODAY I AM GRATEFUL FOR:

NOTES:

NEXT DAY GET AHEAD

DAILY LIFE MAGIC

DATE:

JOY LEVEL

TODAY'S INTENTIONS

REMINDER TO:

QUOTE FOR TODAY

INSPIRED THOUGHTS :

TODAY'S PRIORITES:

EXERCISE:

TOTAL MINUTES:	
TOTAL STEPS:	

WATER INTAKE:

◊ ◊ ◊ ◊ ◊ ◊ ◊

MEAL TRACKER:

BREAKFAST:	LUNCH:
DINNER:	SNACKS:

TO CALL OR EMAIL:

MONEY

MANIFESTED:	GRATEFULLY OUT:

TODAY I AM GRATEFUL FOR:

NOTES:

NEXT DAY GET AHEAD

DAILY LIFE MAGIC

DATE:
(S) (M) (T) (W) (T) (F) (S)

JOY LEVEL

TODAY'S INTENTIONS

REMINDER TO:

QUOTE FOR TODAY

INSPIRED THOUGHTS :

TODAY'S PRIORITES:

EXERCISE:

TOTAL MINUTES:	
TOTAL STEPS:	

WATER INTAKE:

MEAL TRACKER:

TO CALL OR EMAIL:

MONEY

BREAKFAST:	LUNCH:
DINNER:	SNACKS:

MANIFESTED:	GRATEFULLY OUT:

TODAY I AM GRATEFUL FOR:

NOTES:

NEXT DAY GET AHEAD

DAILY LIFE MAGIC

DATE:

(S)(M)(T)(W)(T)(F)(S)

JOY LEVEL

TODAY'S INTENTIONS

REMINDER TO:

QUOTE FOR TODAY

INSPIRED THOUGHTS :

TODAY'S PRIORITES:

EXERCISE:

TOTAL MINUTES:	
TOTAL STEPS:	

WATER INTAKE:

MEAL TRACKER:

BREAKFAST:	LUNCH:
DINNER:	SNACKS:

TO CALL OR EMAIL:

MONEY

MANIFESTED:	GRATEFULLY OUT:

TODAY I AM GRATEFUL FOR:

NOTES:

NEXT DAY GET AHEAD

DAILY LIFE MAGIC

DATE:
(S) (M) (T) (W) (T) (F) (S)

JOY LEVEL

TODAY'S INTENTIONS

REMINDER TO:

QUOTE FOR TODAY

TODAY'S PRIORITIES:

INSPIRED THOUGHTS:

EXERCISE:

TOTAL MINUTES:	
TOTAL STEPS:	

WATER INTAKE:

MEAL TRACKER:

BREAKFAST:	LUNCH:
DINNER:	SNACKS:

TO CALL OR EMAIL:

MONEY

MANIFESTED:	GRATEFULLY OUT:

TODAY I AM GRATEFUL FOR:

NOTES:

NEXT DAY GET AHEAD

DAILY LIFE MAGIC

DATE:

JOY LEVEL

TODAY'S INTENTIONS

REMINDER TO:

QUOTE FOR TODAY

INSPIRED THOUGHTS :

TODAY'S PRIORITES:

EXERCISE:

TOTAL MINUTES:	
TOTAL STEPS:	

WATER INTAKE:

MEAL TRACKER:

BREAKFAST:	LUNCH:
DINNER:	SNACKS:

TO CALL OR EMAIL:

MONEY

MANIFESTED:	GRATEFULLY OUT:

TODAY I AM GRATEFUL FOR:

NOTES:

NEXT DAY GET AHEAD

DAILY LIFE MAGIC

DATE:
Ⓢ Ⓜ Ⓣ Ⓦ Ⓣ Ⓕ Ⓢ

JOY LEVEL

TODAY'S INTENTIONS

REMINDER TO:

QUOTE FOR TODAY

INSPIRED THOUGHTS:

TODAY'S PRIORITES:

EXERCISE:

TOTAL MINUTES:	
TOTAL STEPS:	

WATER INTAKE:

◊ ◊ ◊ ◊ ◊ ◊ ◊

MEAL TRACKER:

BREAKFAST:	LUNCH:
DINNER:	SNACKS:

TO CALL OR EMAIL:

MONEY

MANIFESTED:	GRATEFULLY OUT:

TODAY I AM GRATEFUL FOR:

NOTES:

NEXT DAY GET AHEAD

DAILY LIFE MAGIC

DATE:

(S) (M) (T) (W) (T) (F) (S)

JOY LEVEL

TODAY'S INTENTIONS

REMINDER TO:

QUOTE FOR TODAY

INSPIRED THOUGHTS:

TODAY'S PRIORITES:

EXERCISE:

TOTAL MINUTES:	
TOTAL STEPS:	

WATER INTAKE:

◊ ◊ ◊ ◊ ◊ ◊ ◊

MEAL TRACKER:

BREAKFAST:	LUNCH:
DINNER:	SNACKS:

TO CALL OR EMAIL:

MONEY

MANIFESTED:	GRATEFULLY OUT:

TODAY I AM GRATEFUL FOR:

NOTES:

NEXT DAY GET AHEAD

DAILY LIFE MAGIC

DATE:
(S) (M) (T) (W) (T) (F) (S)

JOY LEVEL

TODAY'S INTENTIONS

REMINDER TO:

QUOTE FOR TODAY

INSPIRED THOUGHTS:

TODAY'S PRIORITES:

EXERCISE:

TOTAL MINUTES:	
TOTAL STEPS:	

WATER INTAKE:

MEAL TRACKER:

BREAKFAST:	LUNCH:
DINNER:	SNACKS:

TO CALL OR EMAIL:

MONEY

MANIFESTED:	GRATEFULLY OUT:

TODAY I AM GRATEFUL FOR:

NOTES:

NEXT DAY GET AHEAD

VISION BOARD

| WEALTH GOAL | HEALTH GOAL |

| LOVE | FAMILY | CAREER |

| BIG PICTURE | KNOWLEDGE |

NOTES:
_____
_____
_____
_____

BOOKS TO READ LIST

✓	BOOK TITLE	AUTHOR	COMPLETION DATE
☐			
☐			
☐			
☐			
☐			
☐			
☐			
☐			
☐			
☐			
☐			
☐			

Life Magic Notes

Life Magic Notes

Life Magic Notes

Life Magic Notes

www.ingramcontent.com/pod-product-compliance
Lightning Source LLC
Chambersburg PA
CBHW040244010526
44107CB00065B/2873